GENDERS

David Glover and Cora Kaplan

LONDON AND NEW YORK

First published 2000
by Routledge
11 New Fetter Lane, London EC4P 4EE

Simultaneously published in the USA and Canada
by Routledge
29 West 35th Street, New York, NY 10001

Reprinted 2001

Routledge is an imprint of the Taylor & Francis Group

© 2000 David Glover and Cora Kaplan

Typeset in Adobe Garamond and Scala Sans by Keystroke,
Jacaranda Lodge, Wolverhampton
Printed and bound in Great Britain by
TJ International Ltd, Padstow, Cornwall

British Library Cataloguing in Publication Data
A catalogue record for this book is available from the British Library

Library of Congress Cataloging in Publication Data
A catalog record for this book has been requested

ISBN 0–415–13491–9 (hbk)
ISBN 0–415–13492–7 (pbk)

CONTENTS

SERIES EDITOR'S PREFACE

The New Critical Idiom is a series of introductory books which seeks to extend the lexicon of literary terms, in order to address the radical changes which have taken place in the study of literature during the last decades of the twentieth century. The aim is to provide clear, well-illustrated accounts of the full range of terminology currently in use, and to evolve histories of its changing usage.

The current state of the discipline of literary studies is one where there is considerable debate concerning basic questions of terminology. This involves, among other things, the boundaries which distinguish the literary from the non-literary; the position of literature within the larger sphere of culture; the relationship between literatures of different cultures; and questions concerning the relation of literary to other cultural forms within the context of interdisciplinary studies.

It is clear that the field of literary criticism and theory is a dynamic and heterogeneous one. The present need is for individual volumes on terms which combine clarity of exposition with an adventurousness of perspective and a breadth of application. Each volume will contain as part of its apparatus some indication of the direction in which the definition of particular terms is likely to move, as well as expanding the disciplinary boundaries within which some of these terms have been traditionally contained. This will involve some re-situation of terms within the larger field of cultural representation, and will introduce examples from the area of film and the modern media in addition to examples from a variety of literary texts.

PREFACE AND ACKNOWLEDGEMENTS

Gender is a vast and expanding subject; in this book we have tried to guide our readers through what seem to us to be some of the most important debates and issues, especially as they impact on culture and representation. Although it is impossible to give a comprehensive treatment of all the cultural and historical aspects of gender in a book of this size, we hope that our discussion will help readers in pursuing further research on those topics which interest them. *Genders* is very much a joint production, conceived together, but the responsibility for the Introduction and Chapters 2 through 5 belongs to David Glover, while Cora Kaplan is the primary author of Chapter 1.

We are grateful to the staffs of the British Library and the London Library for their help with our research for the book. A study leave from Southampton University has allowed David Glover the space to complete his part of the project. Our thanks to John Drakakis for inviting us to write for the series and for his constructive criticism and support, and to Talia Rodgers and Liz Brown who have been enthusiastic and patient editors throughout.

Introduction: gendered histories, gendered contexts

'Gender' is now one of the busiest, most restless terms in the English language, a word that crops up everywhere, yet whose uses seem to be forever changing, always on the move, producing new and often surprising inflections of meaning. We talk about *gender roles*, worry about the *gender gap*, question whether our ideas are not *gender-biased* or *gender-specific*, and we might look for additional information on these and related topics in the rapidly expanding *gender studies* section of our local bookstore. This rich linguistic profusion is confusing enough, but all too frequently it is made worse by the discovery that many of these neologisms appear to be pointing in sharply opposed directions. *Gender role*, for instance, suggests something that constrains or confines, a part we *have to play*, whereas *gender-bending*, by contrast, implies a way out, the subversion of a role through parody or the deliberate cultivation of ambiguity: what was once dutifully thought to be fixed becomes chameleon-like, a part to be played with style, a chance to mock and shock.

As these brief examples show, *gender* is a much contested concept, as slippery as it is indispensable, but a site of unease rather than of agreement. If *gender* is used to mark the differences between men and women, portmanteau words like *gender-bending* or *gender-blending* call those differences into question, drawing attention to the artificiality of what we think of as 'natural' behaviour. This sense of discord ought to warn us against seizing too quickly upon a summary definition of the term, seeking order and clarity where none is to be had. Instead, this introductory chapter will try to explore some of the reasons why gender has become such a vital, but nonetheless intensely problematic word in the contemporary critical lexicon.

OF DOCTORS AND DICTIONARIES

Despite sometimes sounding as if they were mere clichés, little more than the superannuated jargon of interpersonal relations, phrases like *gender role* or *gender identity* are in fact relatively new. Before the Second World War they didn't exist and other closely connected expressions – such as *gender-bender* – did not appear until the early 1980s. The *Oxford English Dictionary* did not begin recording these linguistic innovations until as late as 1989, though its entry for *gender* includes examples that date back at least to the days of Chaucer. To illustrate the early use of the term, consider the following item of gossip from the *Morning Herald*, 29 November 1784:

> The rumour concerning a *Grammatical mistake of Mr.B– – – –* and the Hon. Mr.C– – – –, in regard to the genders, we hope for the honour of Nature originates in *Calumny*! – For, however depraved the being must be, who can propagate such reports without foundation, we must wish such a being exists, in preference to characters, who, regardless of Divine, Natural and Human Law, sink themselves below the lowest class of brutes in the most *preposterous* rites.
>
> (quoted in Chapman 1937: 185)

As it was designed to do, the publication of this story precipitated a scandal in English upper-class circles. The not-so-mysterious 'Mr.B– – – –' was easily recognized as the wealthy young author and Member of Parliament, William Beckford, whom the press accused of entering into what might today be called a homosexual liaison – 'homosexuality' being late nineteenth-century coinage – with the sixteen-year-old son of Lord Courtenay. What really happened remains a matter of dispute, but once the rumour was in print the newspaper attacks rapidly grew bolder and bolder. A little over a week later the veiled language had been dropped and the *Herald* was openly deriding Beckford and Courtenay as 'a pair of fashionable *male lovers'* (Chapman 1937: 186). By the following summer Beckford had yielded to his family's advice and discreetly moved to Switzerland.

Feigning injured piety and outrage at the mischievous rumour-monger, the insinuations in the *Herald's* original report left no doubt as to who was doing what to whom. What made this brief paragraph such a devastating piece of innuendo? In the report's very first sentence the rhetorical reference to 'genders' would have been read as utterly damning, because it plays upon the different connotations of the word current in this period. According to the sixth edition of Dr Samuel Johnson's *A Dictionary of the English Language* (1785), *gender* could refer either to the grammatical practice of classifying nouns as masculine, feminine or neuter; or it could mean 'a sex'. Similarly, the verb 'to gender' meant to produce, to beget, to breed, or to copulate, as in Shakespeare's *Othello*: 'A cistern for foul toads/To gender in.' Thus the 'Grammatical mistake' to which the *Morning Herald* so archly alludes also carries the implication of same-sex desire and points towards the 'crime' of sodomy. This inference is further underscored by the columnist's deft insertion of the verb 'to propagate' and the adjective 'depraved', placing 'Mr.B– – – –' and the 'Hon. Mr.C– – – –' 'below the lowest class of brutes'.

The modern meanings of *gender* still bear the traces of these older historical usages. *Gender* continues to function as a grammatical term, for example, as well as being a euphemism for a person's sex, though it is no longer used as a synonym for the sexual act. So we might be forgiven for thinking that nothing much has changed since William Beckford's time. Yet, compared to today's complex linguistic flux, these eighteenth-century idioms seem remarkably restricted, as if cut off from the perpetual expansion of meaning that characterizes the present.

Part of the reason for this sense of semantic discontinuity stems from the fact that, beginning in the nineteenth century, sexuality gradually assumed a new status as an object of scientific and popular knowledge. The last two hundred years or so have seen what the critic and historian Michel Foucault once described as a 'discursive explosion' around the question of sex, by which he did not simply mean that it came to be talked about more widely or more often or more explicitly, relaxing the grip of repressive conventions or taboos (Foucault 1979: 38). Rather, what really revolutionized sex was the way in which ideas about sexuality began to spread out and touch every aspect of modern social life. According to Foucault:

> The most discrete event in one's sexual behaviour – whether an accident or a deviation, a deficit or an excess – was deemed capable of entailing the most varied consequences throughout one's existence; there was scarcely a malady or physical disturbance to which the nineteenth century did not impute at least some degree of sexual etiology. From the bad habits of children to the phthises of adults, the apoplexies of old people, nervous maladies, and the degeneration of the race, the medicine of that era wove an entire network of sexual causality to explain them.
>
> (Foucault 1979: 65)

Sexuality is here much more than a facet of human nature, the seat of pleasure and desire. It has become a principle of explanation whose effects can be discerned, in different ways, in virtually any stage and predicament of human life, shaping our capacity to act and setting the limits to what we can think and do. The sexual discourses listed by Foucault are astonishingly diverse, ranging from pedagogical discussions on how to teach and discipline children and minors, to medical and psychiatric case studies of disturbed individuals, to treatises on population and demography, and even to ideas about the proper design of buildings, including family houses, dormitories and classrooms.

To see how dramatically thinking about sexuality has changed, let us consider a particularly challenging example, that of a nineteenth-century French hermaphrodite named Herculine Barbin whose memoirs Foucault republished in 1978. Today we would define an *hermaphrodite* as someone who combines features drawn from both sexes: in classical mythology Hermaphroditus, the son of Hermes and Aphrodite, merged with his lover Salmacis to become a being with female breasts and male genitals, after she had prayed to the gods that the two of them might be united for ever. But Foucault's point is that in the Middle Ages and the Renaissance the hermaphrodite's sexual identity was not simply a question of biology: legal, religious and medical codes all had a bearing on how any individual might be treated, and in some circumstances some hermaphrodites could actually choose for themselves whether they wanted to be recognized as a man or as a woman. Not only were the biological facts of the matter subject to interpretation in such cases; more than this, the whole view of human reproductive biology within which these facts were to be understood diverged radically from the dimorphic or two-sex model that seems so obvious to us.

Until at least the middle of the eighteenth century the human body was conceived as being of one flesh: in other words, as consisting of a single, yet capacious sex, an 'open body in which sexual differences were matters of degree rather than kind' (Laqueur 1990: 125). Thus the famous sixteenth-century surgeon Ambroise Paré could write that 'Sexe is no other thing than the distinction of Male and Female, in which this is most observable, that for the parts of the body, and the site of these parts, their is litle difference betweene them, but the Female is colder than the Male' (Paré 1634: 27). Consequently he thought it entirely possible for a woman spontaneously to change her 'sexe' (or, as he put it, 'degenerate' into a man), since 'women have so many and like parts lying in their wombe, as men have hanging forth' and these could certainly be externalized. Paré took such stories very seriously, believing that the only real obstacle lay in the fact that 'a strong and lively heat seemes to bee wanting, which may drive forth that which lyes hid within' (Paré 1634: 975). However, he felt it to be far less likely that men could turn into women, for 'Nature tends always toward what is most perfect and not, on the contrary, to perform in such a way that what is perfect should become imperfect' (Paré 1634: 33).

From the standpoint of twentieth-century clinical medicine this view of sexual difference seems to be incredibly wrong-headed and unenlightened. Yet the story of Herculine Barbin shows that the advances associated with modern anatomy were not without their personal costs. Herculine was raised as a girl in a Catholic orphanage and later worked as a schoolteacher, but, following a medical examination during an illness, she began to have doubts about her sexual identity. A second examination in 1860 led a local court to reverse her civil status and to declare that her 'true sex' was that of a 'young man'. In his medical report Dr Chesnet insisted that, despite all of Herculine's 'completely feminine attributes' including a very small vagina, 'the whole outer part of her body is that of a man'. The conclusive signs of 'the predominance of masculine sexual characteristics' in Herculine were the 'ovoid bodies and spermatic cords . . . found by touch in a divided scrotum', features that Chesnet believed to be 'the real proofs of sex' (Foucault 1980: 123–8). Devastated by this verdict and forced to leave town, Herculine committed suicide in Paris in 1868. In her memoirs she described herself as 'a sad disinherited creature', whose 'very life is a scandal' (Foucault 1980: 93, 99).

In a sense, Herculine Barbin was partly the victim of a new drive to investigate the nature of sexual identity and to catalogue its various anomalies and deviations, a drive which, according to Foucault, reached a peak in France in the decade between 1860 and 1870. Today, the strict anatomical division between the sexes sounds inevitable, mere common sense. According to current medico-legal orthodoxy, whatever a person's sexual tastes may be, it should in principle be possible to classify everyone unambiguously as either male or female. Yet, if one looks at 'sex' from the long-term, historical perspective recommended by Foucault, the fate of Herculine Barbin suggests that to define identity like this is also to close down some of the options that once had been available to those who felt themselves to be 'different'. 'Do we *truly* need a *true* sex?' asks Foucault: after all, isn't what truly matters 'the reality of the body and the intensity of its pleasures' (Foucault 1980: vii).

While the case of Herculine Barbin provides an unforgettably bleak illustration of the extent to which the foundations of sexual knowledge were being thoroughly overhauled in the nineteeth century, this is by no means the full story. Paradoxically, the new modes of medical power and expertise that ultimately made Herculine's life seem no longer bearable also provided the occasion for new voices to make themselves heard, insisting, like the unhappy Herculine, upon the validity and legitimacy of their own experiences. Thus the growing willingness to put 'sex' into question, even to search for the scientific truth about sexual behaviour, gradually opened up new ways in which the entire field of sexual possibilities and sexual identities could be imagined, permanently transforming people's most intimate sense of their sexual selves. 'The nineteenth century and our own' represent an 'age of multiplication', wrote Foucault, an age in which there is 'a dispersion of sexualities, a strengthening of their disparate forms', resulting in nothing less than an 'epoch' of 'sexual heterogeneities' (Foucault 1979: 37).

Nevertheless, Foucault failed to give enough weight to one of the most momentous changes to occur *within* the modern sexual sciences: the recognition that a person's sexual desires cannot be deduced solely from a simple inventory of anatomical facts. This realization was slow in coming, for medical researchers clung to the notion that the human sexual instinct was essentially a physiological phenomenon, initially thought to be localized in the reproductive organs or, on a slightly later view, in the brain's cerebral cortex. Yet in the diagnosis and treatment of sexual abnormalities, the so-called 'perversions' such as sado-masochism, it proved impossible to discover a malfunction in a specific part of the human body that would explain the vicissitudes of the sexual instinct.

We find a profound ambivalence running through the work of writers such as Richard von Krafft-Ebing, the Austrian psychiatrist who first coined the term 'sado-masochism' in 1890. For example, in his massively influential textbook *Psychopathia Sexualis* (originally published in 1886), Krafft-Ebing wavers between asserting that the sexual instinct is rooted in the brain and admitting that there is as yet no clear evidence as to where exactly in the brain it might be. Ultimately, this was a productive contradiction, for it pushed Krafft-Ebing towards the view that sexual behaviour was always bound up with a certain type of 'sexual personality' or 'sexual sensibility'. But he was not alone in reaching this conclusion. Arnold Davidson has shown in great detail how, in the English language, the nineteenth-century word 'sexuality' eventually moved away from its association with the purely biological aspects of 'sex', and came instead to refer to someone's sexual feelings or sexual preferences, reflecting the fact that by the 1890s:

> Sexual identity is no longer exclusively linked to the anatomical structure of the internal and external genital organs. It is now a matter of impulses, tastes, aptitudes, satisfactions, and psychic traits.
>
> (Davidson 1987: 21–2)

These novel meanings crystallizing around the concept of 'sexuality' are a strong indication that sexual life was beginning to be seen as something more than a mere set of sensations: to possess a sexuality was to lay claim to a distinctive form of subjectivity, or what Krafft-Ebing once termed 'mental individuality'. Describing what he called the 'anomalies of the sexual instinct' (such as same-sex desire), Krafft-Ebing claimed that

> These anomalies are very important elementary disturbances, since upon the nature of sexual sensibility the mental individuality in greater part depends; especially does it affect ethic, esthetic, and social feeling and action.
>
> (Krafft-Ebing 1904: 81)

In other words, 'tell me what your desire is and I will tell you who you are' (Foucault, quoted in Macey 1993: 365).

Of course, this cultural shift did not happen overnight, nor did it occur once and for all. Sexual biology and sexual psychology continued to be conflated. Much of the force of Freud's *Three Essays on the Theory of Sexuality* (1905), one of the founding texts of psychoanalysis, lies in his criticism of the widespread belief that achieving sexual satisfaction is 'analogous to the sating of hunger', a straightforward function of the human body (Freud 1977: 7.61). By considering the evidence of 'sexual aberrations' – including studies of homosexuality, fetishism and scopophilia (compulsive sexual pleasure in looking) – Freud was able to reveal the workings of the sexual instinct to be far more complicated than was generally understood. The sheer variety of the sexual behaviour recorded by Krafft-Ebing and the other early sexologists seemed to undermine the assumption that there was any intrinsic, or even natural, connection between the sexual instinct and the object of desire. On the contrary, argued Freud:

> Experience of the cases that are considered abnormal has shown us that in them the sexual instinct and the sexual object are merely soldered together – a fact which we have been in danger of overlooking in consequence of the uniformity of the normal picture, where the object appears to form part and parcel of the instinct. We are thus warned to loosen the bond that exists in our thoughts between instinct and object.
>
> (Freud 1977: 7.59)

To pursue Freud's argument to its logical conclusion necessarily means dislodging 'the normal picture', undermining its customary dominance by seeing it as just one contingent form of sexual desire among many. For Freud, one could almost say, the perversions disclose the truth of heterosexuality.

Although Freud and the majority of the psychoanalytic movement never abandoned the concept of sexual perversion, the line between 'these deviations and what is assumed to be normal' becomes less and less clear as a result of Freud's intervention –

especially since he insisted that there were many situations in which ordinarily acceptable sexual activities such as touching or looking could come to be defined as perverted (Freud 1977: 7.46). It is therefore perfectly plausible to argue on psychoanalytic grounds that 'human sexuality . . . cannot in any sense be enclosed within a specific pattern which may be considered normal'; or, to turn the proposition around, that 'all human sexuality is essentially perverse' (Torres 1991: 73). Similarly, while Freud always stressed that psychoanalysis shared 'a common basis with biology', one effect of his work has been to problematize the relationship between desire and the body (Freud 1979: 9.399). This remains a controversial issue, but for some of Freud's successors the most striking aspect of the *Three Essays on the Theory of Sexuality* is 'the radical loss of the biological' that his argument seems to imply (Laplanche 1976: 125).

Freud's debt to his contemporaries in the field of sexology was considerable. Yet in building upon their work to produce a truer, more scientific theory of sexuality in the *Three Essays*, Freud was also attempting to distance himself from them in order to establish the superior credentials of psychoanalysis, his own distinctive brand of science. For Freud the real interest in studying sexual behaviour lay in its contribution to our understanding of the most inaccessible and troubled regions of mental life; and this meant that he tended to regard sexology as a useful, though ultimately inferior, fact-gathering activity. This spirit of rivalry between the two specialisms has continued down to the present day, but one of the reasons for this tension is that sexology and psychoanalysis obviously overlap. Indeed, Foucault even saw them as being part of the same system of thought, since each is based upon the assumption that the truth about ourselves can be found in our sexual natures. And it is in this area of overlap between sexology and psychoanalysis that we first see the late modern concept of *gender* beginning to emerge.

In the United States especially, the years following the Second World War produced something of a boom for sexology and psychoanalysis. In sexology this phenomenon is best represented by the massive interest aroused when Alfred Kinsey's *Sexual Behaviour in the Human Male* was published in 1948. Although it was an expensive scientific text filled with statistical tables rather than graphic illustrations, Kinsey's book sold 200,000 copies in six months. As with earlier work in sexology, the effect of Kinsey's research was to show how incomplete or misleading popular knowledge about sexuality really was. His findings – like the most widely quoted Kinsey statistic that 'nearly 2 males out of every 5 that one may meet . . . has *at least some overt homosexual experience* to the point of orgasm between adolescence and old age' – not only suggested a sharp divergence between conventional morality and social reality, but they also revealed the inadequacy of existing concepts for describing sexual behaviour (Kinsey *et al.* 1948: 650). It is notable that throughout his work Kinsey tried to avoid using the condemnatory clinical typology of the perversions.

GENDER AND SEXUAL SCIENCE

No one knows precisely when and where *gender* was initially used to refer to the social and cultural aspects of sexual difference, but it is clear that the term was already current in sexology by the early 1960s. For example, *gender* does not figure in Alex Comfort's post-war overview of *Sexual Behaviour in Society* (1950) until the book was revised for publication some thirteen years later (under the new title *Sex in Society*), when the author added a brief discussion of 'gender roles'. Significantly, this was placed in a chapter on 'The Biological Background' to human sexuality, in which Comfort stressed the difficulty in knowing the extent to which our sexual behaviour was instinctive, given 'the far greater importance of higher mental functions in man' than in the other animal species (Comfort 1963: 34). This explains why:

> The 'gender role' which an individual adopts – 'manly' or 'womanly' – according to the standards of his culture, is oddly

> enough almost wholly learned, and little if at all built in; in
> fact, the gender role learned by the age of two years is for most
> individuals almost irreversible, even if it runs counter to the
> physical sex of the subject.
>
> (Comfort 1963: 42)

'Gender' is used here to index the wide variation in styles of
behaviour between societies, but it also suggests that *within* them the
degree of choice is fairly limited. By making his readers aware of
these cultural differences, Comfort hoped to demystify human
sexuality and so help to release them from what he believed were
unnecessary and irrational sexual taboos. At the same time, however,
his more guarded emphasis upon the irreversibility of gender roles
seems to tell against the promise of any easily accessible path to
sexual liberation. For liberal humanists like Comfort it was often
hard to understand why sexual enlightenment should appear to
lag so far behind the other modes of social and technological
progress.

Probably the most thorough attempt to theorize the distinction
between sex and gender in this period is to be found in the writings
of the psychoanalyst and anthropologist Robert J. Stoller, whose
book *Sex and Gender: On the Development of Masculinity and
Femininity* appeared in 1968. Stoller located the starting-point
for his work in Freud's paper on 'The Psychogenesis of a Case of
Homosexuality in a Woman' (1920) which argued that a person's
physical sexual attributes, mental attitudes and objects of desire
could 'vary independently of one another'; so that 'a man with
predominantly male characteristics and also masculine in his erotic
life may still be inverted in respect to his object, loving only
men instead of women' (Freud 1979: 9.398–9). In a similar vein,
Stoller used the term 'gender' to signal the complexities of those
'tremendous areas of behaviour, feelings, thoughts, and fantasies that
are related to the sexes and yet do not have primarily biological
connotations' (Stoller 1968: ix). Not only do we tend to confuse sex

and gender, however. We also assume too readily that the various components of gender are mutually reinforcing, whereas in fact they may well pull in different directions.

In addition to separating sex from gender analytically, therefore, Stoller distinguished between 'gender role' and 'gender identity' in order to indicate that one's inner and outer life may be deeply conflicted or fail to coincide. The gender role that one plays out before others may offer little clue as to who one feels oneself to be, and consequently in Stoller's theory the very definition of gender identity is founded upon the possibility of an inner discord, a kind of non-identity with one's sexual being:

> *Gender identity* starts with the knowledge and awareness, whether conscious or unconscious, that one belongs to one sex and not the other, though as one develops, gender identity becomes much more complicated, so that, for example, one may sense himself as not only a male but a masculine man or an effeminate man or even as a man who fantasies being a woman.
>
> (Stoller 1968: 10)

By the end of this sentence gender identity has begun to sound like a form of alienation and, perhaps not surprisingly, much of Stoller's clinical work was devoted to examining cases in which people felt uncertain as to whether they were 'really' masculine or feminine. According to Stoller the first few years of childhood usually gave rise to a stubborn core of gender identity and this could sometimes clash with subsequent experiences, values or wishes. But such conflicts were rarely simple. In a discussion of those patients whose genital abnormalities meant that they were brought up 'in an atmosphere of parental doubt', Stoller suggested that it was possible for them to develop 'a hermaphroditic gender consciousness', a unique core identity that recognized the division of the world into two sexes, while feeling that he or she was a social and a sexual misfit who 'belongs to neither' (Stoller 1968: 33–4). On the other hand, not all psychic conflicts were necessarily destructive. Commenting on the case of a patient who was a transvestite, Stoller observed that part of the man's pleasure in heightening his sense of femininity through cross-dressing came from a simultaneous awareness of also being male. Here 'the two aspects of gender identity' – 'the later one, *I am feminine*, and the earlier core identity, *I am (nonetheless) a male*' – were equally 'essential to his perversion' (Stoller 1968: 40). To manipulate the limits of gender, to play with and upon a sense of the contradictions of identity, was, for this subject, to secure the conditions of the most intense sexual enjoyment.

The continuing legacy of Stoller's work (and that of the Gender Identity Research Clinic which he set up in Los Angeles in the 1960s) can still be seen in the American Psychiatric Association's official diagnostic manual. There one can find entries on 'gender dysphoria' or 'gender identity disorder', defined as a 'persistent discomfort about one's assigned sex or a sense of inappropriateness in the gender role of that sex', a syndrome that often temporarily affects children – though no clue is offered as to why this should be so (American Psychiatric Association, DSM-IV 1994: 533). While inevitably lacking the psychological subtleties of Stoller's detailed case histories, these brief, abstracted symptomatologies do point up the weaknesses of his own narrowly clinical approach. Stoller had little time for broader social analyses of gender, dismissing Foucault's 'cultural history' of sexuality as nothing more than 'a story', based on 'shards' and 'fragments', that 'leaves out the information that the intimate study of individuals can add' (Stoller 1996: 16–18).

RETHINKING GENDER(S)

As much as any single figure could, Stoller put the distinction between sex and gender on the map for writers and researchers in the humanities and the social sciences. But if his basic ideas quickly became commonplace, they were also soon being used in ways that he could not have anticipated. With the tremendous revival of feminist politics in North America and Western Europe in the late 1960s came renewed attempts to understand and contest the social disadvantages experienced by women and Stoller's separation of sex from gender was pressed into service as the cutting edge of a critique of male domination. So, when Kate Millett began to outline her theory of patriarchy in *Sexual Politics* (1977 [1970]), which was one of the founding texts of second-wave feminism, she drew upon Stoller's work to underscore her argument that 'male and female are really two cultures' since his evidence seemed to cast doubt upon 'the validity and permanence of psycho-sexual identity' as a fact of life. Yet, in staking this claim, Millett was actually moving in quite the opposite direction to Stoller's own highly individualistic psychoanalytic theorizing; for, when she rephrased his distinction to read 'sex is biological, gender psychological, and *therefore cultural*' (my emphasis), she was but one step away from mapping the opposition between sex and gender on to that between *nature* and *culture* (Millett 1977: 29–31).

As we shall see in a moment, there is good reason to question the apparent obviousness of this equation, but it still tends to govern the meanings ascribed to the sex/gender distinction even today. Locating gender within the many-sided realm of culture became the primary means of challenging the supposed inevitability of women's subordination, part of what the historian Joan Scott, looking back over more than a decade of feminist research, has called 'a genuine historicization and deconstruction' of masculinity and femininity that sought to minimize or reduce human biology's capacity to underpin the spuriously 'fixed and permanent quality' of these terms (Scott 1988). 'Gender', according to Scott's pithy definition, is simply 'a social category imposed on a sexed body'. Perhaps the most influential attempt to define the relationship between sex and gender through the contrast between nature and culture occurred within feminist anthropology, notably in Gayle Rubin's 1975 essay 'The Traffic in Women: Notes on the "Political Economy" of Sex'. In a wide-ranging theoretical and cross-cultural analysis, Rubin argued that every known society has what she dubs 'a sex/gender system', that is:

a set of arrangements by which the biological raw material of human sex and procreation is shaped by human, social intervention and satisfied in a conventional manner, no matter how bizarre some of the conventions may be.

(Rubin 1975: 165)

Just as hunger may be satisfied by any number of different kinds of food, each of them 'culturally defined and obtained', so, in any given society, sex too is filtered through the culturally dominant codes that regulate the behaviour acceptable in men and women. But these codes police not only 'the social relations of sexuality'; they also determine the social division between the sexes, the basis upon which men and women are placed into 'mutually exclusive categories'. Pointing to what she saw as the arbitrariness inherent in such classificatory logics, Rubin insisted that:

Men and women are, of course, different. But they are not as different as day and night, earth and sky, yin and yang, life and death. In fact, from the standpoint of nature, men and women are closer to each other than either is to anything else – for instance, mountains, kangaroos, or coconut palms. The idea that men and women are more different from one another than either is from anything else must come from somewhere other than nature . . . Far from being an expression of natural differences, exclusive gender identity is the suppression of natural similarities. It requires repression: in men, of whatever is the local version of 'feminine' traits; in women, of the local definition of 'masculine' traits. The division of the sexes has the effect of repressing some of the personality characteristics of virtually everyone, men and women.

(Rubin 1975: 179–80)

On this view the goal of cultural critique is not only the unmasking of a restrictive and fundamentally flawed conception of nature, but also the liberation of a true, because more genuinely natural, human diversity from the chains of social convention. By clearing away these arbitrary and artificial cultural obstacles, it might even be possible to imagine 'the overthrow of gender itself' – or at least, this prospect seems to be implicit in Rubin's argument (Butler 1990: 75).

Rubin's essay remains one of the most remarkable attempts to think through the causes of gender inequalities, constructing a systematic theoretical framework that links work, kinship and politics. Drawing upon insights from Marxist economics, psychoanalytic accounts of identity and anthropological studies of marriage and the family, Rubin shows how men typically 'have certain rights in their female kin', whereas 'women do not have the same rights either to themselves or to their male kin' and may be used as bridewealth, trophies, gifts and even 'traded, bought, and sold'. Yet the notion that such oppressive kinship systems represent 'an imposition of social ends upon a part of the natural world', including the translation of sex into gender, assumes that sex and nature are somehow unproblematically *given* and exist outside the particular stock of cultural knowledge which makes one society so different from another (Rubin 1975: 175–6).

'Sex is sex,' writes Rubin, 'but what counts as sex is . . . culturally determined and obtained' (Rubin 1975: 165). One of the primary lessons of Foucault's *History of Sexuality*, however, has been that there is no simple sense in which 'sex *is* sex', and that our ideas and beliefs about sexuality have been revolutionized over the last hundred years – indeed, they are still changing. This disquieting observation need not commit us to a naive relativism, a conviction that there can be no such thing as objective knowledge. But it does entail recognizing that what has counted as truth or error has varied enormously over time and that the history of this distinction will always also be a history of those cultural practices such as science, medicine and law within which evidence and proof have been deployed and contested.

Sex and gender are therefore intimately related, but not because one is 'natural' while the other represents its transformation into 'culture'. Rather, *both* are inescapably *cultural* categories that refer to ways of describing and understanding human bodies and human relationships, our relationship to our selves and to others. Sex and gender necessarily overlap, sometimes confusingly so. What once was baldly called a 'sex change operation' is now, not entirely euphemistically, known as 'gender reassignment', a term that reflects the growing instability of the body's contours in many contemporary societies, its increasing malleability or openness to reinvention, whether through drugs, dress, discipline or surgery. Of course, there are limits to who or what we might become, though these are not always the limits we might expect. In English law, for example, regardless of how much one's body may have changed its shape or form since birth, it is not currently possible to alter one's legal status from male to female, or vice versa. In this respect, legality – and not, as Freud once wrote, 'anatomy' – is destiny.

As a rough approximation we might say that 'sex' is the name we give to the language through which we speak and come to know our desires, while 'gender' denotes the cultural practices or cultural media that enable these desires to be played out. In her important book *Gender Trouble*, Judith Butler has argued that gender is a symbolic form of 'public action' whose recurrence allows for our recognition as desiring and desirable subjects. For Butler:

> gender is an identity tenuously constituted in time, instituted in an exterior space through a *stylized repetition of acts*. The effect of gender is produced through the stylization of the body and, hence, must be understood as the mundane way in which bodily gestures, movements, and styles of various kinds constitute the illusion of an abiding gendered self.
>
> (Butler 1990: 140)

According to Butler's theatrical metaphor, gender is fragile, provisional, unstable, the sum total of its appearances rather than the expression of a unifying core. Masculinity or femininity come in many transient guises, all of them in some measure unfinished or incomplete. And this is as true *historically*, when one considers the range of competing definitions of what it has meant to be a man or a woman, as it is true *individually*, when one remembers the difficulties in growing into and sustaining an identity. 'Thus,' as Freud noted, 'we speak of a person, whether male or female, as behaving in a masculine way in one connection and in a feminine way in another' (Freud 1973: 2.147). Yet he failed to add that we also disagree among ourselves as to what is appropriately masculine behaviour in one case or acceptably feminine in another.

Butler's claim that gender is primarily an act of signification or representation can sound as if gender is a matter of choice, of picking up and discarding identities at will. Butler has herself cautioned against this popular, but deeply misguided reading of *Gender Trouble*:

> The bad reading goes something like this: I can get up in the morning, look in my closet, and decide which gender I want to be today. I can take out a piece of clothing and change my gender, stylize it, and then that evening I can change it again and be something radically other, so that what you get is something like the commodification of gender, and the understanding of taking on a gender as a kind of consumerism.
>
> (Kotz 1992: 83)

The flaw in this picture, says Butler, lies in its failure to take into account the contradictory mode in which we inhabit our sense of gender, not as an identity that we freely embrace, but one that we also struggle against, that sustains us at the same time as it constrains us. Like the everyday use of language from which it partly derives, gender underpins our capacity to make decisions and act upon them, while constantly slipping out of our control and ensnaring us in complex webs of meaning that no single individual can ever hope to master.

But the false image of the subject who selects her gender for herself is at least correct in suggesting that there are many genders. So various are the different conceptions of masculinity and femininity that emerge from the miscellany of sites and settings in modern societies, that we can justifiably refer to them in the plural as *masculinities* and *femininities* (see Connell 1987; 1995). How wide is the range of variation within and between these genders? The answer to this question will largely depend upon contingencies of time and place, but nevertheless critics have continued to disagree about how the problem should be theorized. Thus Teresa de Lauretis has claimed that today's representations of gender are produced by a number of distinct 'technologies of gender' such as cinema or advertising and that we, as gendered subjects, can be seen to be 'constructed across a multiplicity of discourses, positions, and meanings, which are often in conflict with one another' (de Lauretis 1987: x). For de Lauretis these discursive contradictions may actually provide a breathing space, a moment in which new gender identities might begin to be fashioned. By contrast, though writing in roughly the same period and starting from similar analytic assumptions, Chantal Mouffe has argued that 'despite their heterogeneity, discourses and practices do not take place in isolation' but interact with one another to create 'a common effect'. As a result 'the feminine' is invariably set up 'as a subordinated pole to the masculine', a process in which 'the symbolism linked in a given society to the feminine condition plays a fundamental role' (Mouffe 1983: 141). There can be no alleviation of gendered inequalities unless this symbolism is successfully confronted.

GENDER AND LANGUAGE: WITTIG'S PRONOUNS

As an even more fundamental example of how gender has become a contested term, consider the work of the French writer Monique Wittig. Wittig combines the roles of radical feminist theorist and novelist and her work has been principally concerned with problems of gender and language. At first sight her ideas seem to be sharply at odds with the central argument being developed in this book since, not only does Wittig fail to pluralize gender, she also insists that it is an inherently singular term. This is because linguistically 'the masculine is not the masculine but the general' – that is to say, the use of words like 'mankind' or 'he' to refer to men and women alike perpetuates an abstract, universalizing idiom that is denied to women, making men its sole beneficiaries (Wittig 1992: 60). From Wittig's perspective the consequences of this much-overlooked fact are devastating.

Wittig's position is rooted in a materialist theory of language, according to which concepts and symbols are not mere free-floating ideas or signs, but have real effects upon individual subjects. Despite her indebtedness to Marxism – she refers to it at one point as 'the science which has politically formed us' – Wittig explicitly turns the Marxist theory of revolution on its head. Instead of adopting Marx's argument that the conflicts produced by economic forces will bring about a political revolution which will necessarily destroy the dominant 'categories of language', Wittig calls for a revolution in language as the first condition of social change:

> Can we redeem *slave*? Can we redeem *nigger, negress*? How is *woman* different? Will we continue to write *white, master, man*? The transformation of economic relationships will not suffice. We must produce a political transformation of the key concepts, that is of the concepts which are strategic for us. For there is another order of materiality, that of language, and language is worked upon from within by these strategic concepts.
>
> (Wittig 1992: 30)

For all its high-flown rhetoric, passages like this are in deadly earnest, since they point to language's overwhelming impact 'upon the social body, stamping it and violently shaping it' (Wittig 1992: 78). While some people have been forced to conform to established ideas about what is and is not natural, others have been written out of history.

Wittig's prime target is what she calls 'the straight mind', a mode of thinking about the world that 'cannot conceive of a culture, a society where heterosexuality would not order not only all human relationships but also its very production of concepts and all the processes which escape consciousness, as well' (Wittig 1992: 28). On this view, gender relations can never be equalized, for the categories of 'man' and 'woman' are defined as asymmetrical or hierarchical from the outset. Language plays a crucial role in sustaining this imbalance, for by learning to call oneself a woman one is also implicitly deferring to the privileges enjoyed by men. By installing a basic division at the core of our being, the heterosexual imagination denies women the capacity to act as subjects, something that can only be achieved by taking control over the ways in which language is used. To become what Wittig calls a 'total' or whole subject one must first break with the assumptions embedded in the grammar of heterosexuality, that system of linguistic positions which conventionally assigns women an identity only in relation to men. Of course, there have always been those who have slipped through the nets of language, those whose 'refusal to become (or remain) heterosexual always meant to refuse to become a man or a woman, consciously or not' (Wittig 1992: 13). It logically follows, in the words of one of Wittig's most famous slogans, that 'Lesbians are not women', a conclusion which she is delighted to accept (Wittig 1992: 32).

But how is it possible to transcend the prison-house of language in order to bring about the abolition of gender? And isn't Wittig herself inescapably complicit with those same linguistic resources that enable her to diagnose her condition and make her arguments intelligible to others? It is here that we turn to Wittig's practice as a novelist, and also return to the grammatical meanings of gender with which we began this chapter.

Gender has often been used primarily as a sociological category, as if language were only of secondary importance. Reversing this assumption, Wittig looks to the place within language where gender begins: the personal or subject pronouns *I, you, he, she, we, you, they*. These markers are 'the pathways and the means of entrance into language', the words that position us within discourse as male or female, 'working in the same way as the declaration of sex in civil status' by calling upon specific gendered identities (Wittig 1992: 78–9). Wittig's extraordinary fiction takes the personal pronoun as its point of departure, foregrounding the principles by which they operate and attempting to disrupt their normal functioning. In her first novel *L'Opoponax* (1964), for example, Wittig explores the interior world of a young schoolgirl, creating a curiously distanced stance through the use of the indefinite or ungendered French pronoun *on* (the English 'one') in her narration, interspersed with the protagonist's name, Catherine Legrand:

> On ne met pas de pantalon quand on est une petite fille. On n'aime pas ça parce qu'on devient deux. Catherine Legrand mais aussi ce qui est dans le pantalon et qui n'est pas exactement Catherine Legrand. Peut-être Catherine Legrand est la seule petite fille à porter un pantalon et à n'être pas exactement une petite fille.
>
> (Wittig 1964: 17–18)

> You don't wear knickers when you're little. You don't like them because they divide you in two, Catherine Legrand but also what is in the knickers which is not exactly Catherine Legrand. Perhaps Catherine Legrand is the only little girl who wears knickers and who is not exactly a little girl.
>
> (Wittig 1979: 13)

Especially in the original French, the effect is radically to unsettle the formation of identity, to interrupt the implied reference linking pronoun and proper name, suggesting that Catherine Legrand cannot quite occupy the *elle* (or 'she') that is traditionally awaiting her, just as her underclothes and her selfhood don't sit comfortably together, somehow failing to add up. Moreover, as Wittig has herself noted in a commentary on this text, *on* is a marvellously elastic word that can be made to stand for any number of persons: *I, you, they, everyone*. And, insofar as it is able to invoke all of these at once, identification is always on the move, impossible to pin down. When, towards the end of the novel, a new and seemingly more decisive note is struck, signalled by an abrupt shift of pronoun – 'Je suis l'opoponax' (I am the opoponax) – there is no corresponding gain in clarity, for Catherine has earlier written that the mysterious opoponax, from which the book takes its title, cannot be described, being 'neither animal nor vegetable nor mineral, in other words indeterminate'/'ni animal, ni végétal, ni minéral, autrement dit indéterminé' (Wittig 1964: 161, 207; 1979: 119, 154).

Wittig's fierce desire to push identity to its outermost limits, to transcend the categories through which identity has traditionally been thought, to disengage identity from gender, and to enact a new form of subjectivity within literary language places considerable demands upon her readers, preventing them from holding on to the binary logic that oppressively couples men and women together. This linguistic disruption is intensified still further in her later books. In *Les Guérillères* (1969), for instance, Wittig makes extensive use of the rather specialized French collective pronoun *elles*, which has always taken second place to the masculine *ils*. *Elles* can only be used to refer to a group of women, whereas a mixed group is invariably referred to as *ils*, even when the women outnumber the men. Moreover, *ils* has an important generalizing function that is denied its feminine counterpart, for it can also mean *they* in the sense of *people* or *mankind*, whereas *elles* cannot. Wittig's strategy is to elevate the feminine plural to the same status as the masculine *ils*, to make it resound with a sense of communal destiny and purpose. 'Word by word,' comments Wittig, '*elles* establishes itself as a sovereign subject', forging a new collectivity in an epic struggle, a *nous*, a 'we' who have proved themselves to be true 'camarades' and who together finally sound the funeral march for those who died for freedom, 'un air lent, mélancolique et pourtant triomphant' (Wittig 1992: 85; 1969: 208).

At one point in *Les Guérillères*, *elles* specifically reject the vocabulary of their adversaries, their enemies in language, the masculine 'ils', who have dismissed their fight as a 'revolte contre nature' (Wittig 1969: 153). So, in line with this repudiation, the text scrupulously avoids making reference to 'men' or 'women', since in Wittig's lexicon these words are tokens of capitulation. As we have seen, Wittig's textual manoeuvres are not easily reproduced in translation: the 'you' of the English version of *L'Opoponax* is gender-free, but suggests a closer, far more familiar idiom than the original *on*. And in the case of *Les Guérillères* the unavailability of a gendered alternative to 'they' led Wittig's translator to replace *elles* by 'the women', a substitution that wholly subverts the author's own avowed intentions.

Nevertheless, Wittig's fiction is a good example of the way in which fiction can serve as a laboratory for the exploration of gendered modes of consciousness, including those we might imagine to be among its terminal forms. Novels such as *L'Opoponax* and *Les Guérillères* stand in a long line of modernist texts whose stylistic innovations foregrounded the whole question of gender, power and subjectivity, and whose authors have included Gertrude Stein, Dorothy Richardson and Virginia Woolf, among many others. Though very different from Wittig's *guérillères*, the protagonist of Dorothy Richardson's multi-volume novel *Pilgrimage* (1915–38), Miriam Henderson, has been described as 'one of the first women in fiction to be shown *other* than in relation to a man' (Beauman 1995: 153). And, as Jeanette Winterson's *Written on the Body* (1992) shows, we have by no means seen the last of those wily, ambiguous narratives that persistently avoid framing themselves in exclusively masculine or feminine terms.

Wittig's prose-poetry, her uncompromising experimentalism informed by an intransigent belief that 'everything is socially constructed', represents an invitation to rethink the meaning and boundaries of our genders (Fuss 1989: 41). In the following chapters we take up this challenge, focusing initially upon the making of femininity and masculinity, before moving on to those more obliquely gendered margins that are often treated as 'threats to heterosexuality' or even 'threats to gender itself', but which have typically been lived out in the lengthening shadow of legal or extra-legal prohibitions and sanctions (Butler 1997: 135). If our identities are partly fictions, cover stories set in place by the narratives within which our lives are intertwined, then the restless play of identifications that our reading or viewing releases can become one of the key ways in which these fictions can be re-scripted. 'When we let ourselves respond to poetry, to music, to pictures,' writes Jeanette Winterson, 'we are clearing a space where new stories can root, in effect we are clearing a space for new stories about ourselves' (Winterson 1996: 60).

1

FEMININITY AND FEMINISM

In the opening pages of 'Femininity', the fifth of his *New Introductory Lectures* (1933), Sigmund Freud poses the 'riddle of the nature of femininity' as an unresolved question that 'people have knocked their heads against' throughout human history. Commiserating with one sex and winding up the other, Freud goes on, tongue-in-cheek, to separate and gender the subjects and objects of the interrogation: 'men' it seems have not 'escaped worrying over this problem' but 'to those of you who are women this will not apply – you yourselves are the problem' (Freud 1973: 146). Yet as Freud knew very well, women had been 'worrying' over the problem of 'femininity' at least as long as men. For although femininity may be defined as a set of attributes ascribed to biologically sexed females, what exactly those attributes are, and the extent to which any given version of femininity is natural or cultural, have been debated long and hard by women themselves. When, for example, Charlotte Brontë's heroine, Jane Eyre, speaks passionately to the reader of the gendered division of emotions: 'Women are supposed to be very calm generally: but women feel just as men feel', she is challenging the commonsense understanding of femininity in the 1840s, and, by implication, its scientific as well as its social basis (Brontë 1987: 96). In life as well as in fiction, one *can* both 'live' a gendered identity in all its complexity, and hold its received definition at arm's length. In fact, the analysis of femininity by women has a long pedigree in its own right. Later in the chapter we will turn to some key moments when femininity was under particular pressure and scrutiny, exploring them through both women's fiction and feminist theory and criticism.

Before we come to that history we may need to remind ourselves of how easily femininity in its everyday use naturalizes and genders so many other terms. In 'Femininity' Freud asked his readers to reconsider their automatic association of passivity with women, and activity with men. He points out that it is 'inadequate . . . to make masculine behaviour coincide with activity and feminine with passivity. . . . Women can display great activity in various directions, men are not able to live in company with their own kind unless they develop a large amount of passive adaptability.' 'Even if,' he argues, one were to say that psychologically femininity gave preference to 'passive aims', 'a passive aim may call for a large amount of activity.' He warns his readers that to give activity and passivity crude gender alignments serves 'no useful purpose and adds nothing to our knowledge' (Freud 1973:148–9). The opening theoretical move in 'Femininity' is to suggest not only that the conventional binaries that designate gender are convenient but mistaken social fictions, but that all humans are potentially bisexual – that their choice of sexual object is the result of an often impeded and difficult psychic trajectory. Whether the emphasis is on gender or on sexuality, Freudian theory makes femininity an outcome not an origin. We might add that to be a 'woman', biologically, psychologically and socially, is not necessarily to be thought 'feminine' in whatever local and customary sense that may be understood. A promiscuous qualifier, 'feminine' can and does attach itself to almost anything: cats, cars, colours, handwriting, home furnishings – and men. Yet as an aspiration or an accolade, a despised or wished for descriptor, 'feminine' always evokes 'woman'.

It is not uncommon, of course, to hear women described as 'unfeminine'; supposed coldness, aggression, ambition, neglect of children or high intelligence can quickly bring this accusation upon them. But even so-called unfeminine women are inscribed, we might argue, with a femininity, if not always the one most valued by a particular culture. Femininity, the noun, is never quite the sum of its adjectival parts, which are in any case likely to be in conflict. The saucy flirtatiousness of a pleasure-loving young woman and the selflessness of the devoted mother – to take two common stereotypes – may both be considered 'feminine' qualities, but they have historically been seen to belong to very distinct stages of a woman's life trajectory. Mothers and prostitutes, little girls and old crones, women of different classes and ethnic identities and sexual orientations – all these supposedly discrete 'types' of the female – may be thought to 'have' femininity, but both within one lifetime and between social and cultural differences the cluster of attributes thought to make up their gendered identity may vary widely. And while we may first of all see masculinity and femininity as defined through their complementarity and opposition, it is equally important to see them as internally divided and moralized: versions of 'good' and 'bad' femininity – blondes and brunettes; mothers and prostitutes; white women and black women; straight and lesbian; middle-class and poor – have also been set up as binary terms. While femininity is always associated with femaleness it has been a common racialist strategy to ascribe feminine traits or femininity to non-white or other supposedly inferior ethnic groups as a whole. The men in those groups in particular – the Irish, Jews, Asians, Native Americans and Africans have all been so depicted – although what marks these men as feminine varies from supposed excesses of feeling to passivity to a degree of nurturance thought inappropriate in Anglo-Saxon masculinity. Homosexual cultures have their own rhetorics of 'masculine' or 'feminine' traits and behaviours, and value them differently than the homophobic and heterosexist societies that observe them. In the twenty-first century femininity persists as a contradictory constellation of meaning that can refer at once to normative, flawed and even 'perverse' categories of the human. That is why it is perhaps more useful to think of femininity in the plural – femininities – and to see femininity both as an umbrella term for all the different ways in which women are defined by others and by themselves, and as a semi-detached property of the self, not identical with the biologically sexed body. Indeed in its most removed but perhaps most ubiquitous sense femininity is a trope – 'luck be a lady tonight' – the figurative bearer of meanings that may only have a contingent and metaphorical relationship to 'woman'.

All these uses of femininity are interconnected, and their interface is most often their contradictory evocation of femininity as at once sexual, transgressive, even threatening, and as inferior, weak and dependent. Does 'lady luck', we might ask, reward the gambler by her propriety or her compliance? When, for example, Virginia Woolf opens a 1927 essay on 'The Art of Fiction' with the conceit 'that fiction is a lady and a lady who has somehow got herself into trouble' she makes just such an oblique metaphorical use of femininity, playing knowingly with the kinds of 'trouble' that women, and even 'ladies', might get into or up to, and so conjuring up the cultural misogyny that such a situation might invoke, while mocking, at the same time, the archaic chivalry of male critics: 'gentlemen' who 'have ridden to her rescue' (Woolf 1992: 121). Woolf's essay was written in the decade that British women were given the vote, a decade in which their new access to civic freedom was constantly attacked in the media for encouraging women's independent, and therefore promiscuous, exercise of their sexuality. Questions of gender and sexuality are especially difficult to prise apart when femininity is under discussion. Elaborating her metaphor, Woolf explores the plight of fiction through other, less risqué, stereotypes of the feminine. Fiction, she argues, has been unfairly and condescendingly seen as the 'humble' domestic drudge or dependent wife of the arts, unaesthetic, 'feeble' and a 'parasite' (Woolf 1992: 124). The trope of femininity gives Woolf a flexible weapon with which to attack the lapses and prick the pretensions of literary criticism, but it is a weapon that can easily turn on its wielder. The figurative strategy of 'The Art of Fiction' depends on the prevalence of the cultural misogyny which it both invokes and derides, deflecting in passing the chauvinism that might greet the woman critic and writer herself.

Woolf was, on the whole, an optimist when it came to the future of gender politics, but reading her literary and feminist essays now reminds us how tenacious have been the attitudes that she described. The more that formal legal and civic discrimination against women in the public sphere have been eroded in the West, the more clearly we can see the shadow that persistent cultural misogyny still casts over women, a shadow that often seems longer and darker precisely in relation to the advances and rising expectations that legislative equality has achieved. These negative associations of inferiority and worse, which so stubbornly cling to the subjective and objective representations of woman, have been one of feminism's strongest *raisons d'être*, but they have also provoked its most strenuous theoretical disagreements. Feminism continues to argue about what is natural or biologically given and what is culturally constructed; it remains divided, although perhaps less absolutely so than in the past, about how to analyse the psychic and the social components of female subjectivity. (Indeed, as with sex and gender, the divide between the social and the psychic is never hard and fast.) One recurring strand of feminist analysis of femininity has highlighted the supposed female virtues of social sympathy and nurturance, seeing in femininity an enlarged capacity for supportive human relations with caring motherhood at its centre. Lynne Segal writing in 1987, worried that the increasing fragmentation of the women's movement and its social and political agendas had allowed the conservative idea that female difference should be understood as both natural and desirable a heightened attraction that ironically threatened to become the new '"common sense" of popular feminism' (Segal 1987: 2). Nevertheless a strong majority among feminist theorists have been sceptical about linking femininity to those feelings and practices that have long been associated with innate gender difference and which have historically determined women's subordination, preferring to see most aspects of gender as potentially mutable and ripe for reinvention. And even the bleaker interpretations of femininity past and present, those which emphasize oppression rather than resistance, have also provoked feminism's innovative, utopian imagining of the future of gender. When women have considered the 'problem' of their gender, they have drawn on both analytic pessimism and creative optimism. Over the past two centuries women have, in their writing, visual art and music, developed a rich cultural account of femininity and affect, an archive from which one might derive a critical history of gendered feeling. It is unlikely, however, that all feminists would be in agreement about its theoretical underpinning, or its highs and lows.

A poignant vignette that shows the contrasting moods in which such a history might be written opens Ann Snitow's now classic 1989 essay 'A Gender Diary' which reflects on one of modern feminism's central paradoxes: the 'need to build the identity "woman" and give it solid political meaning and the need to tear down the very category "woman" and dismantle its all-too-solid history' (Snitow 1990: 9):

> In the early days of this wave of the women's movement, I sat in a weekly consciousness raising group with my friend A. We compared notes recently: What did you think was happening? How did you think our lives were going to change? A. said she had felt, 'Now I can be a woman; it's no longer so humiliating. I can stop fantasizing that secretly I am a man, as I used to, before I had children. Now I can value what was once my shame.' Her answer amazed me. Sitting in the same meetings

during those years, my thoughts were roughly the reverse: 'Now I don't have to be a woman anymore. I need never become a mother. Being a woman has always been humiliating, but I used to assume there was no exit. Now the very idea "woman" is up for grabs. "Woman" is my slave name; feminism will give me freedom to seek some other identity altogether.'

(Snitow 1990: 9)

What the postwar women's movement had done, Snitow suggests, was to take what had seemed natural, imposed and inevitable, freeing up gender identity, redefining it as unstable and mutable, making it open to forms of choice, which she describes as 'subtle psychological and social negotiations about just how gendered we choose to be' (Snitow 1990: 9). 'Negotiation' is, she implies, the diplomatic and liberating sequel to a more violent and less voluntary experience of femininity. Snitow's exemplary conversation with her friend hints at a future for gender where choice not prescription would rule. But it also highlights something more recondite and more particular to women: the 'shame' and 'humiliation' through which many western middle-class women in the latter half of the twentieth century had come to experience their lived and imagined gender. Shame and humiliation are powerfully negative emotions to describe the subjectivity of women who were, after all, enfranchised, educated and ever increasingly entering the professions, even if they still remained in a very disadvantaged position in comparison with white middle-class men. Some feminist writers have appropriated the term abjection to theorize these negative feelings, pinpointing the interaction between the ways in which societies and women themselves too often conceive of femininity. Abjection's ordinary meaning denotes being thought inferior, either by oneself or by others, something unworthy and vile, or less than human, something to be cast out; for feminist psychoanalysts, like Julia Kristeva, abjection marks out a landscape of feeling by and about women that places them before, below and beyond culture – almost outside what can be represented within it. The evocation of abject feelings by women themselves hints at something stubbornly intractable in the negative inflection of femininity, something not easily shifted by the removal of legal, political and economic impediments to equality. Yet even this residual negativity serves as a galvanizing force, a motive for further exploration and analysis of just what makes female gender such a difficult identity. If the desires of Snitow and her friend to embrace or disavow their gender mirror opposite choices, once choice became an option, what drew them together, what perhaps drew them into feminism, was their common acknowledgement of the degraded value of femininity both 'out there' in the dominant culture and in their own psychic life.

The mix of abjection and euphoria that is the psychic condition of modern femininity, and which fuels contemporary feminism, can be thought of as a creative paradox rather than as pure contradiction or simple complement, for the tension between these opposed psychic states has been productive rather than otherwise. Feminist historian and theorist Joan Scott has argued that paradox is constitutive of feminism itself from the eighteenth century onwards. She borrows the self-definition of Olympe de Gouges, author of the *Declaration of the Rights of Woman and Citizen* (1791), as 'a woman who has only paradoxes to offer and not problems easy to resolve' to describe feminism itself, both then and now (Scott 1996: 4). As Scott reminds us, 'paradox' implies not only a term that may be both true and false at the same time, or a statement that is resistant to dominant ideas, but also a linguistic balancing act that is generative of poetic meaning (Scott 1996: 4). Paradox is therefore an immensely suggestive way of posing the 'riddle' or the 'problem' of femininity, perhaps especially as it confronts the lopsided relationship between female subjectivity and the universal concept of the human. Denise Riley has suggested that we think of femininity as a part, not the whole of female subjectivity, whether collective or individual. 'There are differing temporalities of "women", and these substitute the possibility of being "at times a woman" for eternal difference on the one hand, or undifferentiation on the other' (Riley 1988: 6). For:

> any attention to the life of a woman, if traced out carefully, must admit the degree to which the effects of lived gender are at least sometimes unpredictable, and fleeting. . . . Can anyone fully inhabit a gender without a degree of horror? How could someone 'Be a woman' through and through, make a final home in that classification without suffering claustrophobia? To lead a life soaked in the passionate consciousness of one's gender at every single moment, to will to be a sex with a vengeance – these are impossibilities, and far from the aims of feminism.
>
> (Riley 1988: 6)

The recognition that one need not be a woman all of the time in all aspects of one's life at best throws open a world of transformative possibility and creative potential and at the very least poses femininity as a part-time occupation for full-time humans. Yet this very realization can be a catalyst and prelude for women – like Snitow's friend – to confess to powerfully negative emotions about being female, characterized by that combination of despair and degradation that comprises abjection, or the horror* and claustrophobia that Riley says accompany the feeling that one is trapped into always being a woman. Such feelings erupt as women simultaneously try to live up to perceived social models of femininity and attempt to deny, resist or cast them off. Writing from a more psychoanalytic perspective than Snitow, Scott or Riley, but in other ways not at odds with their emphasis on the mutability and instability of gender, Jacqueline Rose asks us to think about 'femininity' as part of the necessary 'division and precariousness of human subjectivity itself' (Rose 1986: 52). Rose presents this as a question *about* identity rather than an answer to it, one that expresses a desire that cannot, and perhaps should not, be met. She interprets Freud's exploration of femininity's riddle as a double question, the second more searching than the first: 'how does the little girl become a woman, or does she?' (ibid.: 45).

How to analyse – and perhaps to smooth – the imperilled psychic path from infancy to female adulthood has been a vexed issue for feminism ever since Mary Wollstonecraft, in *A Vindication of the Rights of Woman* (1792) turned her reader's attention to the way in which 'females . . . are made women of when they are mere children' (Wollstonecraft 1988: 117). Wollstonecraft argues that women are made, not born:

> Every thing that they see or hear serves to fix impressions, call forth emotions, and associate ideas, that give a sexual character to the mind.
>
> (Wollstonecraft 1988: 117)

In her writing we find a detailed and extended account of the social construction of gender, as she resists Jean-Jacques Rousseau's claim that femininity is an instinctive set of sexed traits. But Wollstonecraft also, as Barbara Taylor has argued, saw the psyche as creative precisely in its capacity to fantasize, to wish for and invent different scenarios for gender, while believing, at the same time that women were especially vulnerable to the seductive erotics of romantic narrative, and prey to dangerous and self-destructive imaginings (Taylor forthcoming).

From the late eighteenth century forwards fantasy, conscious and unconscious, occupies a contested and contradictory position in feminist thought – the sign, on the one hand, of the sway of the irrational, and on the other, in the more respectable guise of 'imagination', of the vitality of creativity and radical thinking. Femininity has historically been seen in terms of the difference between men and women's affective, emotional life, and this supposed division of affect becomes surrounded by new medical evidence as the scientific model of anatomical sexual difference moved from what historian Thomas Laqueur has called the 'one-sex/flesh model' of the period prior to the Enlightenment to the 'two sex/flesh model' which comes to dominate nineteenth-century science and medicine (Laqueur 1990: 8). The historical inter-dependency of theories of mind and body makes it especially hard to distinguish where sexuality might end and gender begin.

As some aspects of the biological bases of gender inequality came under increasing critique in the twentieth century, feminists have given renewed attention to the way in which women's mental and emotional life has been theorized. In the past twenty-five years a debate among feminist theorists both about the origins of femininity and, more generally, about the meaning of mental life, has focused on whether that distinctively modern 'science' of psychoanalysis has helped or hindered an understanding of sex and gender. From the late 1960s, the first years of the 'second wave' of the women's movement, American feminists such as Kate Millett led the assault on Freud's view of femininity. Millett's witty attack in *Sexual Politics* (1970) makes Freudian psychoanalysis the whipping boy for the general misogyny of the dominant culture. Other feminist writers, following Millett, held Freud responsible for the normalizing and conservative use to which his theories had been put by both therapists and cultural analysts. The analyst's abuse of power in the patient–analyst relation, when men were the analysts and women the analysands, has been seen to exemplify patriarchal relations. Worst of all, psychoanalysis was portrayed as a theory that drew universal assumptions from the evidence of very local and historically specific cultures, 'fixing' gender by suggesting that psychic structures were somehow outside of or immune to cultural influence and thus denying the possibility of historical change.

Countering this wide-ranging critique, which nevertheless tended to exaggerate both the role and influence of psychoanalysis, and to misinterpret its object of study, mental life, as a totalizing theory of subjectivity, other feminist theorists have defended both the historical intervention of psychoanalysis and the useful-ness of its paradigms in understanding femininity. An early and groundbreaking study, Juliet Mitchell's *Psychoanalysis and Feminism*

(1974) argued that Freud's view of women was more suggestive and less reductive than that of other psychoanalysts of his time. Mitchell contends that those analysts, Karen Horney and Ernest Jones among them, who set out nobly to amend Freud's 'unfriendly' view of women, found themselves positing female difference ever more distinctly as a separate and unequal identity, grounding it in gendered concepts of instincts and desire. Jacqueline Rose, in an important essay, 'Femininity and its Discontents' (1986 [1983]) points out that Freudian theory consistently queried those dominant interpretations of women's mental life that had become increasingly medicalized and pathologized by the late nineteenth century. While feminists in the 1970s focused their debate on psychoanalysis around its concepts of sexual difference, Rose argues that they neglected the most important contribution of psychoanalysis to feminism – its theories of the unconscious. Through the unconscious and its symptoms – dreams, slips of the tongue, jokes – psychoanalysis has emphasized the incoherence, difficulty and discontinuity in *all* human identity. In his work on femininity between 1924 and 1931 argues Rose, Freud moved from focusing on the little girl's meditation on her difference from little boys and its possible violent sources, '("injury", as the *fact* of being feminine), to an account which quite explicitly describes the process of becoming "feminine" as an "injury" or "catastrophe" for the complexity of her earlier psychic and sexual life ("injury" as its *price*)' (Rose 1986: 91). The work of Jacques Lacan, Rose continues, extended and deepened Freud's emphasis on a human psyche 'always and persistently divided against itself' (92).

Psychoanalysis, like feminism, has, from its origins, put the issue of normative ideas about gender high on the list of its internal disagreements. We would highlight here its productive insights for feminism, not least its recognition that femininity and masculinity are identities which must always, in some sense, *fail*. Feminists, such as Rose, who hold this position do not imagine that there should or can be a psychically smooth and unproblematic path to 'stable' gendered identity, for it is precisely the belief in such a path that naturalizes gender and sexuality, and offers it up to regulation. They are suggesting instead that the radical potential of feminism is in its emphasis on the unstable, contradictory and paradoxical nature of *all* social and psychic identities. Even within this general position, writers remain divided about which psychoanalytic thinker – Freud and Lacan are the two most often cited – offers the most persuasive critique of fixed or stable identity.

The feminist debate on psychoanalysis has been important, not least because the disagreements within feminism about the character and future of femininity are part of those epistemological and political questions about truth and agency that have become the subject of a much larger set of social and political debates which ask whether there can be an objective, universal ground for knowledge when so many categories of people are excluded from its making. Is a fixed and positive sense of self always the precondition for being a successful actor in the world, or is agency, the ability to take actions on behalf of oneself or one's group, a more complex concept? As Rose pointed out in her essay on femininity, psychoanalysis paradoxically stands accused of being both a normative, regulatory discourse and one that disables feminist agency through its insistence on the instability of identity. Theories of gender and sexuality are valued or attacked for their ability to encourage or undermine forms of social and political action, as if such action flowed in a simple and unidirectional way from how we understand the grounds of difference. To caution against such vulgar causal arguments is not to suggest that theories are free from politics, but only that the politics of their construction and their deployment are never singular, but always part of a complex constellation of ideas and practices that are specific to different times, places and societies. Within western feminism in the past quarter century quite opposed theoretical positions on femininity have come together in alliances around particular campaigns of action about reproductive rights, nuclear power and pornography. Conversely, in a particular conjuncture a theory of difference may offer liberation and inspire rebellion for one group, while implying that others should by the same token remain subordinate. In the following three sections we will show how this occurs by exploring two historically specific moments in the history of femininity.

'WOMEN FEEL JUST AS MEN FEEL': FEMININITY AND FEELING 1790–1850

When historians explore the evolution of 'modern' ideas of gender, the eighteenth century is usually seen as the time when changes start to accelerate. Certainly from its last decades onwards femininity is a busy category, performing, in Mary Poovey's useful formulation, a great deal of 'ideological work' in western culture, involved in the making and unmaking of theories of gender (Poovey 1988:2). Frequently employed as both an indication and a cause of the uneven development and alarming dynamism of whole societies, femininity is always Janus-faced, read by the dominant culture and by the feminism that seeks to defend and change it as at once a residual symptom of the inequalities or virtues of past cultures and as a sign, good and bad, of things to come. In *A Vindication of the Rights of Woman* (1792) the republican and feminist Mary Wollstonecraft uses these past and future tenses to strategic effect. She invokes the Gothic and feudal to describe imperilled femininity, picturing the bourgeois women for whom she is writing as prisoners of a threatening and abusive power, literally and metaphorically 'immured in their families, groping in the dark' (Wollstonecraft 1988: 5), or even worse, in the case of her heroine Maria, in *The Wrongs of Woman* consigned by her husband to a madhouse. Husbands and families may be timeless adversaries for women, but in *A Vindication* Wollstonecraft associates what she sees as women's internal enemies, their narcissism, dependency and deference, with the worst aspects of an immoral and oppressive aristocratic culture whose residual feudalism was under attack at the moment of democratic revolution in which she was writing. But, as Harriet Guest has argued, Wollstonecraft in *A Vindication*, as well as elsewhere in her writing, also figures feminine sensibility, or feeling, in terms of the modern market economy, which in turn is characterized by a gendered division of labour (Guest 1996: 3–4).

Emotion is a key element in every definition of femininity in this period: what woman is or can be is interpreted in terms of the perceived difference between women's and men's feelings. The lines of race and class that divide women themselves are marked by distinctions of feeling also: humanist and democratic arguments at this time need to assert what is not deemed to be apparent, that all women have maternal emotions. In the late eighteenth century, sensibility and sentiment are the operative categories of feeling that women must negotiate. While some critics see little distinction between sensibility and sentiment, it is useful to distinguish them. Sensibility refers to those emotions that seem instinctive or physical, rather than the discourse of moralized sentiment. Sensibility in women can be a dangerous force, easily corrupted; it can fire the utopian imagination or derail or deform its purposes. Guest argues that in the 1790s the 'dreams of sensibility' that surface in the work of writers like Wollstonecraft and her radical contemporary, the novelist Mary Hays, were 'peculiarly appropriate for the articulation of the . . . need to reform the social and political condition of women, and particularly middle-class women'. The 'language of sensibility', says Guest, 'links the feminine pursuit of financial and moral independence with the masculine pursuit of professional ambition' for it is a language which 'takes advantage of the blurred public and private character of professional or commercial ambitions, which for men, as well as perhaps for women, are the phantoms of libidinised pursuit, of an idea of self-fulfilment which is as much about the desires of the private and sexual subject as it is about the more thoroughly moralised aim of independence' (Guest 1996: 19). As a result Guest explains, women's self-positioning at this moment is profoundly paradoxical, for even when highly politicized 'feminine subjects' in the 1790s, like Hays and Wollstonecraft, conceived 'of themselves in terms of discourses of politics, of the division of labour, of civil and commercial culture' they must both reject those divisions insofar as they excluded women and accept them as a regime which would allow them to be agents in modern culture. New, reformed and liberated femininity had simultaneously to accept the terms of the market – including the volatile feelings that were its psychological drivers – and abjure them. Women from this period onwards, seeking more rights and more freedom, had little choice but to move within the emotional and libidinal economies of market societies, which demanded self-realization and the up-front desires that went with it. These were the conditions and contradictions under which femininity and feminism were to develop (Guest 1996: 20).

These problems were taking self-conscious shape for feminist writers in the 1790s. They surface again in a somewhat different form in early Victorian Britain, when gender along with other forms of difference and hierarchy is once more being challenged at a time of social and political unrest. The 1840s, like the 1790s, was a particularly turbulent time in British and European societies with economic recession exacerbating class conflict in Britain. The threat of revolutionary uprising at home as well as its reality on the continent undoubtedly contributed to the anxious edge that one finds in women and men's writing about gender and sexuality. Most of the novels of the 1840s and 1850s that put the working-class Chartist movement for political rights overtly or covertly at the centre of their plots – Benjamin Disraeli's *Sybil* (1844), Elizabeth Gaskell's *Mary Barton* (1848) and *North and South* (1855), and Charlotte Brontë's *Shirley*, were all engaged in one way or another with the pleasures and dangers of women in public roles, as Chartist supporters (Sybil), as poor working women and prostitutes (*Mary Barton*), or cross-dressing landlords (*Shirley*). Each of these fictions end conventionally with women happily ensconced in marriage and under male protection, but their concern with women outside the home in defiance of gender norms is woven into their mixed sympathy and unease with working-class subjectivity and the threat of violence implicit in the political orchestration of collective discontents among the poor. This ambivalence is highlighted in Elizabeth Barrett Browning's 'novel-poem', *Aurora Leigh* (1996 [1856]), the story of a woman poet, in which feminism, femininity and working-class resentment and rage are also brought together in a narrative where poetry, not social revolution, becomes the preferred solution to class divisions. Mary Poovey has suggested that in this period anxiety about 'women's aggressiveness', social and sexual, is 'managed . . . through a series of substitutions' (Poovey 1988: 12). In the proto-feminist texts of the mid-nineteenth century, humiliation and degradation as well as aggressiveness – those disturbing feelings that all humans are subject to, must be shifted away from the aspiring heroine. In *Aurora Leigh* working-class women are either an underclass of foul-mouthed slatterns who have neither filial nor maternal feelings, or idealized, deferential victims such as the seamstress Marian Earle; they represent in both cases the extreme ends of the spectrum of possible femininities, incarnations of anger and abjection, those excesses of feeling which the bourgeois woman poet is at pains to dissociate from her own identity.

Perceived racial difference which relied on similar economies of emotion to make its distinctions provided another figurative strategy through which femininity could be fractured and hierarchically ordered. The 1840s was also the first full decade after the abolition of slavery in Britain, a decade which shows a steady decline in humanitarian sympathy with ex-slaves who were now no longer the objects of pity but potential equals and competitors in the world labour market and in other spheres also. This too is reflected in novels by women that are centrally concerned with the limits and possibilities of femininity. In Charlotte Brontë's *Jane Eyre* (1987 [1847]) and Dinah Mulock Craik's *Olive* (2000 [1850]), the post-slavery revision of social hierarchy is represented by threatening, violent racialized women from the West Indies: the mad wife of

Rochester, Bertha Mason in Brontë's novel, and the mixed race mother–daughter pair, Celia and Crystal Manners, in *Olive*. The fury these women express at men and women from the privileged, white British culture is at one level a narrative symptom of the complicated response that British writers in the 1840s made to the legacy of colonial slavery. More immediately, perhaps, the unacceptable anger of British women against the gendered division of emotion and labour that condemned them both to calmness and inaction was, in these novels, displaced into the rage expressed by racialized 'foreign' women against both imperial masculinity and femininity.

Gender, but especially femininity and its proto-feminist revisions, in this early Victorian period has, interestingly, been the site of impassioned critical debate in the second half of the twentieth century, as if the trope of emotion that structured the theory and representation of femininity in the nineteenth century itself has acquired a second life in its critical reconstruction in our own time. In her writing about gender in the 1840s and 1850s Mary Poovey has designated certain resonant issues in the period which 'had the potential to expose the artificiality of the binary logic that governed the Victorian symbolic economy' as '"border cases"'. Border cases 'mark the limits of ideological certainty' and were the site of 'intensive debates', Poovey believes, because they 'threatened to challenge *the* opposition upon which all the other oppositions claimed to be based – the opposition between men and women' (Poovey 1988: 12). In turn we might see the intensity of recent debates about gender in Victorian Britain as just such a modern 'border case', but one whose ideological stakes are somewhat different. Modern feminists critics use the Victorian period to revisit the unresolved issues of what kind of opposition gender is, and what kind of ethics and politics can be assigned to 'traditional' femininity, but they are posing these questions in the context of another one that has long divided feminists: is gender, in fact, the only or primary 'founding' opposition?

While there is an unprecedented mass of social, political and medical discourse in this period which focuses on what femininity should or should not be, recent criticism has given the novel a particular prominence and influence as the space where both gender and genre are under revision: femininity's story as imagined in early Victorian novels by women is identified as the avatar of a new kind of fiction. Writing in the 1960s and 1970s, cultural critic Raymond Williams saw the 1840s as a kind of watershed decade for masculinity and femininity, arguing in particular that these years saw a deepening division between the emotions thought proper for men and women to display. Men's tears, Williams suggests, became a sign of unmasculine weakness rather than of proper masculine sensibility. Such a cultural shift away from expressive masculinity, Williams believed, meant that imperilled femininity (the female orphan in contemporary fiction is his example) came increasingly to represent the generic plight of 'man alone' (Williams 1965: 84–5). For Williams the appearance of such an icon is a tragic effect of modernity: the female orphan stands for the anomie and misery of the alienated psychic life of men and women in industrial societies where communal feeling has been destroyed. When the female orphan represents only herself and her gender, she is no longer a tragic hero. Williams argued that women's writing, especially the work of Charlotte Brontë, and her orphaned heroines, Jane Eyre or Lucy Snowe of *Villette*, introduces into the novel and the culture as a whole, a distinctively new subjective voice, whose self-representation is both feminine and sinister. This voice, at once 'private' and 'individual', is the confessional and desiring voice of the quintessentially modern subject, the voice of an unrestrained and asocial individualism which elevates private feeling above public good (Williams 1984: 70). But if for Williams the predicament of the proto-feminist heroine of the 1840s represents a wider crisis of modernity, its remedy or compensation, the development and celebration of mental and emotional life – what some theorists call the invention of human 'interiority' – as they are expressed within the narratives created by women writers is seen as false and dangerous.

Williams's view of women's writing is, by implication, challenging a perspective that praises the individual and the private, at the expense of the social and communal. Indeed, his reading of gender in the 1840s is soon overtaken by an influential strand of feminist criticism from the 1970s which unambiguously aligns itself with the proto-feminist protagonists of this period and their authors, seeing both as pioneering forerunners of late twentieth-century bourgeois women heroically struggling against the limitations of marriage, exclusion from public life and the still active double standard of sexual morality. The female orphan in this staging of a feminist analysis does not stand in for a universal subject, but is emphatically the emblematic victim and potential agent of her sex. These early and important feminist studies, especially Elaine Showalter's *A Literature of Their Own* (1978) and Sandra Gilbert and Susan Gubar's *The Madwoman in the Attic* (1979), delight in women's personal ambitions and transgressive desires where these fictions actually endorsed them; it is more often the conventional resolutions of marriage and motherhood that they must justify to late twentieth-century women readers. For them the women writers were not the vanguard of self-referential and selfish materialism, but resistant minority voices, exemplary rebels for their time in what they saw as an unfinished democratic revolution.

By the 1980s, when the euphoria of the early years of feminism was on the wane, this initial body of work on nineteenth-century women's writing was being subjected to revision within feminism (mirroring wider disagreements in both activism and scholarship) for its failure to take account of the class biases and the racist and imperial assumptions embedded in the novels and authors it championed. Gayatri Chakravorty Spivak in a groundbreaking 1985 essay 'Three Women's Texts and a Critique of Imperialism' asks feminism to think again about the politics of *Jane Eyre*, which, she argued, had become the 'cult text' of a feminist individualism that was neither reflective nor critical about the less progressive implications of its political investments (Spivak 1985: 263). A later essay by Susan Meyer, '"India Ink": Colonialism and the Figurative Strategy of Jane Eyre', traces the complex racial representations and identifications which subtend the creation of Jane as moral protagonist and survivor, showing how Brontë manipulates racial tropes both to support Jane's resistant identity and final emergence as white wife and mother (Meyer 1996). In a fascinating and influential study, *Desire and Domestic Fiction: A Political History of the Novel* (1987), Nancy Armstrong uses the work of Michel Foucault to elaborate and extend the gist of Williams's argument as part of a debate within feminism. She sees the novel itself, in the eighteenth and nineteenth centuries, as 'containing the history of sexuality within it', by which she means the history of gender as well (Armstrong 1987: 204). Its most innovative development was the invention of an interior psychic world which Armstrong figures as feminine. Both the desiring femininity she describes, and the novel itself, are personified as appetitive and acquisitive; indeed the novel's 'omnivorous' form means that 'there is very little cultural material that cannot be included within the feminine domain' (204). The writing of the Brontë sisters is key to Armstrong's analysis. The ideological work that she ascribes to 'domestic fiction' generally – fiction by women in the eighteenth and nineteenth centuries that centres on the private, subjective sphere of life – was to transform 'political information', implicitly gendered masculine, into 'psychological information' which then becomes the province of a new kind of femininity. Even where the targets of Charlotte Brontë's criticism are demonstrably social, such as the hypocrisies and abuse that are practised by the Governors of Lowood school for female orphans which Jane Eyre attends, Armstrong argues that Brontë substitutes the wrongs of woman for the wider injustices of class: 'she displaces class conflict onto sexual relations' (200).

Although strongly critical of the immediate and long-term effects of Victorian women's fiction, Williams and Armstrong, by arguing that the new femininities articulated in the domestic novel altered the form and content of Anglophone fiction for ever after, gave these novels and their authors what could be interpreted as a flatteringly central role in the making of modern literature and culture. However, this supposed power comes with an ethical price tag that is too high in any accounting, for it portrays the femininity constructed by early Victorian women writers as endowed with an exaggerated and malign agency in the making of the modern self, an argument it would be difficult to sustain if we looked at a wider range of discourses on gender and identity. Such an argument also depends on a paradoxical logic in which the critic makes an ethical and political judgement about what kind of questions properly belong to the public arenas of debate. By insisting that issues of gender, sexuality and psychic identity belong to the private sphere, and therefore cannot be 'political', this analysis reproduces in theory the very divisions between private and public, personal and political, that are the object of its critique. As a result the psychic life of humans, or their 'interiority' as it is sometimes called, is represented as the invention and inherent property of a powerful but pathologized femininity. In this analysis, psychic selfhood becomes not the place where we all dream, but modernity's bad dream about itself, a dream with material effects that can do infinite social and cultural harm.

Armstrong's depiction of the feminist femininity of the 1840s has the advantage of rejecting two over-simple characterizations: the received image of passive, repressed and victimized Victorian womanhood *and* its replacement, the celebratory portrait of vanguard egalitarian feminism, painted by liberal feminists of the 1970s. But her monstrous alternative to abject or heroic womanhood is as unidimensional as these earlier formulations. Should feminism accept the mantle of the begetter of modern fiction, if the price is that it is held responsible for the death of progressive politics? Neither accolade nor accusation seems quite deserved. Nor does the division of public and private inscribed in this analysis bear much relationship to the way in which early and mid Victorians themselves saw those issues, for while conservative social commentators of both sexes advanced the view that ideal femininity conformed to 'natural and instinctive habits' of women, 'love, tenderness and affectionate solicitude' for children, spouses and parents, such moral qualities were at the service not just of men as individuals, but of men as 'citizens' (Gaskell 1972: 165). The state was, as it still is, invested in particular articulations of femininity which supported it. The 'private' in which middle-class femininity was supposed to reside might have been the daily business of maternity, marriage and domestic life, but in ideological terms such femininity, conceived as a set of emotional attributes, did highly public work. We might think of femininity in this sense as a kind of fiction of political calculation, a double entry, as it were, in the ledgers of social accountancy. Certainly the women and men who defended or criticized the separation of spheres knew this very well: it was femininity's function as the mainstay of nation and state through the affective relations of the family that they were debating.

In fact, femininity in the 1840s might best be seen through the lens of Guest's complex discussion of the 1790s. In the 1840s as in the 1790s the political aims of women for more cultural power and for economic and social parity in the public sphere, as well as their other aspirations and wishes – for passion, marriage and motherhood – draw on an affective vocabulary in which the desiring languages of the market and those of the gendered self are hard to disentangle. While both women and men vigorously critiqued the ways in which the coldly instrumental mores of capitalism were shaping both masculinity and femininity and affective life – Dickens's *Dombey and Son* (1982 [1847]) is just such a polemic against the corruption of love and family feeling under the pervasive influence of the market and the desires it unleashes – men's texts tend to resolve these issues unambiguously in favour of the exclusion of women from all but the domestic and the maternal. Excluded or participant, women's agency or subordination was emphatically a public matter, and a social one. For women writers, in any case, supporting the relegation of women to domestic life was rarely if ever without contradiction. Their own practice as authors undermined the solutions that the many last chapters which release their heroines from paid employment or cultural production into blissful domesticity provided. Women's novels in the 1840s imagined women who made a broad claim for the right to desires of different kinds – 'all the incident of life, fire, feeling', as Jane Eyre puts it – although their narrative closure often settled for much less (Brontë 1987: 95). In Jane Eyre's famous soliloquy from the rooftop of Thornfield just cited, we can see how Brontë's refusal of a gendered division of feeling is the basis of her rationale for a femininity that went beyond the matrimonial or domestic. When Jane declares that 'Women are supposed to be very calm generally: but women feel just as men feel; they need exercise for their faculties and a field for their efforts as much as their brothers do; they suffer from too rigid a restraint, too absolute a stagnation, precisely as men would suffer', she makes her case through the language of public, masculine sensibility, the driving language of approved masculine ambition (Brontë 1987: 96). But most women writers were criticizing the excesses of that sensibility as well as asserting a right to it. The desires and priorities of industrial and commercial masculinity were, they thought, in need of reform, and Gaskell and Brontë both allow the reader and the female protagonists to see the world created by it through the eyes of its economic and social victims. Thus, like Wollstonecraft and Hays, but more opportunistically, since she draws on without ascribing to their republican politics, in *Jane Eyre* Brontë aligns the suppression of women's feeling at one point with the situation of the 'rebel slave' and the disempowered generally, provocatively implying that the imposition of 'stillness' and 'tranquillity' on women could spark a rebellion comparable to the 'political rebellions' that 'ferment in the masses which people earth' (ibid.).

We have been arguing, throughout this section, that a key element in understanding femininity and its discontents from the late eighteenth century to mid-nineteenth century is the gendered rhetoric of feeling and its deployment. As we suggested earlier, the discourse of feeling is intimately bound up with the way in which the expanding sciences of the human increasingly differentiated men and women's physiology. Historian of science Nancy Stepan goes further in arguing that the developing models of sexual difference were interactive and interdependent with the theories of racial difference then being elaborated (Stepan 1990). Skin colour, body type and hair as well as reproductive organs were the physical markers of such differences, but their social meaning was expressed in terms of emotional attributes, capacities and dangers. The language of feeling however was not, as certain critics suggest, the sole property of a newly invented private individual exclusively gendered female, but shared its terms with the discourses of the market that it sometimes resisted and critiqued, as well as with those of the state and nation that it wished to reform and support. When women in the mid-nineteenth century tried to break down the arbitrary divisions of the emotions that culture set in place and theorized as natural, they defended their transgression by splitting femininity itself across class and racial lines and displacing transgressive emotions into women of lower status. Yet this self-protective move never quite works. Jane Eyre's defiant soliloquy is preceded by a defensive challenge directed less at the reader than at the gathered opinion of the whole world: 'Anybody may blame me who likes, . . . Who blames me? Many, no doubt; and I shall be called discontented' (Brontë 1987: 95). This pre-emptive antici-pation of blame cannot quite deflect the warning to be meted out for demanding emotional and social equity. For Jane's meditation is soon interrupted by the sinister and threatening sound of female laughter and the 'eccentric murmurs' and 'oral oddities' (96) at first wrongly ascribed to the drunken working-class servant Grace Poole, but later correctly identified as the ravings of Rochester's wife, Bertha

Mason, the 'white' Creole, whose unchaste appetites prefigure her descent into madness and her transformation into a racialized creature with 'fearful blackened inflation of the lineaments' (Brontë 1987: 249), without gender or human attributes. The feared punishment for Jane's desire for equality of feeling and opportunity is averted, narratively speaking, by subdividing the female self and projecting its excesses on to degraded and racialized femininities.

The core statement of Brontë's polemic – 'women feel just as men feel' – strikes at the heart of all arbitrary divisions of affect among types of humans; yet its very radical implications seem to provoke in the challenger herself the immediate need to re-establish the threatened binary by asserting the differences of class or of race. If one is asking, as feminist criticism and theory of the 1980s and 1990s has done, whether the eighteenth- and nineteenth-century origins of modern Anglophone feminism, or the femininities that statement advanced, were politically and ethically progressive by late twentieth-century standards, the answer is sure to be no. Yet the understanding of those ethics and politics through a deeper exploration of the history in which they were embedded is of the utmost interest and importance to us today, not least because that fearful reflex which reinstates the differences it seems to challenge is by no means behind us. But the questions themselves are best posed and answered theoretically in a form that does not replace the historical distinction between good and bad femininity with an equivalent distinction between feminism's misguided past and its progressive present. Such a distinction implicitly assumes that feminism today can stand completely outside and remain untainted by the political forces of market, state and nation. History suggests otherwise.

FEMININITY BETWEEN WORLD WARS

'Always to be a governess, always to be in love' is how Virginia Woolf, writing of Charlotte Brontë in 1916, characterized (and caricatured) both Brontë's best known protagonist and the subordinate, monotonous and emotionally static femininity of the Victorians. For Woolf, Brontë is emphatically not the precursor of twentieth-century modernity or modernist literary forms, but the exemplary prisoner and victim of a femininity and a fictional aesthetic that must be superseded. Between Brontë who died in 1855 and Woolf, whose writing career began in the early 1900s, lies almost a half century of struggle to advance women's rights, and challenge restrictive and misogynistic representations of women. English-speaking feminism was a fully fledged movement by 1916, with a leading cause, the vote, and an embattled but highly visible profile on the political scene. From the 1880s onwards men and women writers and social thinkers fashioned a new, liberated femininity – a vanguard identity dubbed the 'new woman' – that demanded parity with men in every sphere, and a new masculinity to go with it. But while the First World War hastened the granting of the franchise in Britain, the underlying beliefs in gender difference and women's inequality proved much harder to shift. The 'femininity' that early twentieth-century feminists were determined to uproot and replace was more than a century old and harder to supplant than had been supposed. Woolf's frequent evocations in her feminist writings of the thwarted lives of early Victorian women writers, rather than of those born a little later who, like George Eliot, were more unconventional, suggests, rightly we think, that many women between the wars still lived with and under the restrictions that were associated with a much earlier period. Yet in spite of the uneven development of women's emancipation, there is no doubt that the war proved a catalytic moment for gender as for other social hierarchies, and in its wake women's fiction, and feminism too, shifted its ground and altered its narratives, with some surprising results in how they imagined femininity.

We will be looking at a range of these fictions, and will be focusing especially on the way in which class and race construct femininity between the wars, a period when writers of all kinds experimented with formal and philosophical innovation. We began this chapter with Freud's provocative essay, 'Femininity' because, as we have argued, psychoanalysis was the site of some of the most novel theorization as well as the most intense and interesting disagreements about the meaning of identity and gender difference. As a discourse which claimed to have a new truth about psychic life and sexuality, it can be seen as in a kind of covert competition with fiction, with which it shared some of the same ambitions. Psychoanalysis becomes a common referent in the fiction of the interwar years, a signifier of new and 'modern' ideas about the self in everything from Agatha Christie's detective fiction to Dorothy Richardson's experimental 'stream of consciousness' novels. Fiction's view of psychoanalysis is rarely friendly, but the novel's theorization of gender, and perhaps especially femininity, betrays some of the same contradictions and uncertainties that we find in Freud, his followers, and his psychoanalytic adversaries. One way of approaching Freud's 'Femininity' and other writings on the same subject in this period is to place them in the context of the imaginative writing by women in the interwar years, approaching psychoanalysis not as an orthodoxy in the making but rather as a discourse that was part of a spectrum of analytic and speculative texts on gender – and women in particular – in this particularly volatile period in the history of gender.

In Britain women were granted the vote in two stages – at age thirty in 1919 and at twenty-one only ten years later. In that crucial decade the media discussion of the 'flapper' franchise, about the dangers of letting unmarried twenty-something women vote, and therefore play an official role in civil society, acts as a touchstone for new and daring discussions of what 'woman' could mean or be, as well as provoking a strong backlash against the supposed freedoms they might take. Femininity's supposed excesses included the rampant expression of women's sexuality and the rejection of what was recognizably feminine: politicians remarked that even women didn't seem to want to be women any more. Virginia

Woolf's feminist manifesto, *A Room of One's Own* (1929) argues that the resentment and anger, as well as the abjection, that were, she believed, the psychic companions of the restrictive femininity of the Victorians, would soon fade away. Her playful, gender-bending fiction, *Orlando* (1928) is, as Rachel Bowlby puts it in her introduction to the novel, 'a "what if", a serious fantasy which imagines what femininity (or, for that matter, another masculinity) might be in quite different conditions – if anything were possible' (Woolf 1992: xlvi). As Orlando enters the twentieth century, Woolf allows her to be a woman, to have children and a husband and a career, for Woolf believed optimistically in the transformation of femininity, as to a great extent did most of her generation of women writers, although only a few of them would have identified with her outspoken feminism.

We can see this re-imagining of femininity attempted in fictions that were less obviously experimental than *Orlando*, such as Elizabeth Bowen's *The Last September* (1929), a novel set in 1920 among the aristocracy in an Anglo-Irish country house during the guerilla war between the British Army and the IRA. Marda Norton, a cosmopolitan 29-year-old visitor, teases the restless, orphaned Lois Farquar who is just emerging from her adolescent dependency on her aunt and uncle. Urging Lois impatiently to some form of independent action, Marda asks her why she continues to live with her relatives. Lois answers: "'I like to be in a pattern . . . I like to be related; to have to be what I am. Just to *be* is so intransitive and so lonely.'" "'Then you will like to be a wife and mother'", Marda responds ironically, adding, "'It's a good thing we can always be women.'" "'I hate women'", Lois replies fiercely, "'But I can't think how to begin to be anything else . . . I would hate to be a man. So much fuss about doing things'" (Bowen 1998: 98–9).

Lois's problem – her creative paradox – is how *not* to be a woman in the mould of her aunt or her dead mother, or alternatively, how not to envy or identify with the too busy or prematurely vitiated masculinity of her uncle, family friends, cousin or suitor. Bowen describes with peculiar poignancy Lois's desire to steer instead a path of independence that has not yet been charted. To be 'a woman', from Marda's perspective, is an identity of last resort, a safety net that she herself is probably choosing, as, after breaking off a series of engagements, she heads resignedly towards a pragmatic marriage. Lois's half-formed fears and desires are represented in a more philosophical vein. Bowen gives the adolescent a rather lofty set of anxieties in making her afraid of the 'intransitive' isolation of just *being*; more positively but conservatively she values and needs that relatedness so often associated with femininity, but she also longs for an identity outside the forms of the domestic heterosexuality linked to the social pieties of her upper-class upbringing. Resisting but also embracing the clichés of masculine freedom, 'She did not want adventures, but she would like just once to be nearly killed', she reaches clumsily for a heightened experience of life that has analogies to the sublime – an aesthetic confrontation with what is terrible and frightening – one that is neither marked by femininity nor by the familiar tropes of bourgeois culture and leisure (Bowen 1998: 99). In deliberately ambiguous but telling phrases, Bowen describes Lois as wanting to see 'backgrounds without bits taken out of them by Holy Families' and hungering to visit 'unmarried sorts of places' (99). Not unlike Woolf's Orlando, she 'thought it would be pity to miss love' (99). Indeed, Lois's sense of the constraints of her gender does not amount to the full rejection that her fierce 'I hate women' implies, but is more to do with the way class determines the visibility and status of women, for while she 'did not mind being noticed because she was a female, she was tired of being not noticed because she was a lady' (99).

At the same time as Lois strains against the inhibitions and prejudices of her class as it shapes and controls her femininity, she is unconsciously its bearer. When she thinks of travel abroad she thinks of Cook's, the travel agent of the well-to-do, arranging her itinerary and booking her seats – a gentle, joking reminder from the well-born Irish Bowen that there were social limits to Lois's imagination and her rebellion. These limits inhere in the writers themselves; for all the boldness with which interwar women writers in the United Kingdom offered their heroines and their readers a chance to fantasize femininity otherwise, in their narratives new femininities are, in very overt ways, mediated by and through class relations, and in less obvious ways by the exclusions of both empire and race. 'Everything mocked', was Woolf's intended motto for her proposed fiction, *Orlando*, yet this *jeu d'esprit* on gender mocks least of all the author's own love affair with the idea of aristocracy; for its renegade androgynous protagonist, affectionately modelled on her friend and lover Vita Sackville-West, permission and privilege are intertwined. Jaime Hovey has argued that the Sapphism of *Orlando* – its subtextual celebration of lesbianism – is represented through racialized tropes of transgression. In *Orlando* Woolf locates her most negative versions of femininity – its sentimentality, its conventional heterosexuality, and its implied social and political conservatism – in caricatures of nineteenth-century domestic servants, who themselves are made to stand in for the Victorian middle class, including Britain's bourgeois monarch, while a more buoyant, perverse and adventurous version of female subjectivity is reserved for the upper classes.

Woolf's double move in *Orlando* is to celebrate a certain kind of transhistorical aristocratic identity in which the tie to the landed estate permits the destabilizing of gender, so that Orlando can, albeit not at his/her own volition, *be* alternately a man and a woman. Such a move challenges, if only obliquely, that long tradition reaching back to the eighteenth century in which middle-class women writers – and Woolf, born into the London intelligentsia, is emphatically one of these – targeted aristocratic femininity as both over-privileged and corrupt, placing the advancement of women's rights and the progressive future of both women and the nation confidently in the hands of the expanding middle class. The interwar years witnessed a kind of imaginative rebellion by women writers against what is seen to be complacent and provincial in both bourgeois femininity *and* bourgeois feminism, a rebellion which, in fiction at least, transfers to Britain's titled and historic class, together with the group just below it, the landed gentry or 'squirearchy', an oddly vanguardist role in the transformation of gender, considering that this class was generally seen as declining in social, economic and political power.

We have suggested how this revision of class femininity functions in *Orlando*, and in *The Last September*. It is also thematized in Daphne du Maurier's hugely popular *Rebecca* (1938). Alison Light suggests that the 'desire to be differently female is central to du Maurier's best-known novels' (Light 1991: 166). At first glance, *Rebecca* might seem to be a novel in the anti-aristocratic tradition of earlier proto-feminist women writers, focusing like Brontë's *Jane Eyre* on the literal and figurative demise of masculine aristocratic privilege, in this case Maximilian de Winter's inherited estate, Manderley. Yet as Light has argued, while *Rebecca* pushes the demonization of upper-class femininity as far is it could go, stigmatizing the beautiful, accomplished Rebecca, de Winter's dead first wife, as sadistic, sexually perverse and diseased, the 'overkill' in the narrative attack on Rebecca 'testifies to the extraordinary power and fascination' of the novel's images of 'sexual anarchy' (178). It is true that the humble, nameless middle-class heroine who becomes de Winter's second wife, is gradually disabused of her desire to envy or emulate the aristocratic woman she has replaced; indeed, the novel approvingly charts her progress from a repressed and easily intimidated child-wife into a woman who is at least her husband's equal. Even so Rebecca is by far the most interesting character in the novel; her amorality and contempt for men and their desires seductively invites identification from the reader. Rebecca, as an idealized and feared construct of the second wife's imagination, represents in Light's analysis 'the insecurity at the heart of all femininity,' but Manderley, that Tory, English stronghold is also 'a place in the imagination where a freer and more independent sexuality might have been possible' (178). Du

Maurier explicitly exposes Rebecca's heterosexual infidelity, and hints darkly if euphemistically at her possible bisexuality. Yet the novel's open homophobia is directed less at Rebecca than at Manderley's housekeeper 'Danny' Danvers, whose passion for her dead mistress is represented as both creepy and murderous. Nevertheless, the seductive wickedness of its dead protagonist, her entirely transgressive but wonderfully active femininity, overrides the conventional ethics that the novel espouses and seriously erodes the reader's sympathetic alliance with the tiresomely insecure second wife. As if to emphasize the pleasures of excess Max de Winter's estate is itself endowed with an exotic, out of order femininity. In *Rebecca*, Light suggests, du Maurier allows her readers a temporarily dangerous alliance with outrageous femininity, and, if they so wish, a safe rejection of it. While Manderley burns, in a conflagration lit by Danny, the vengeful custodian of Rebecca's memory, consuming in its flames the comfortable future of its proprietor and his young wife, it returns, at once longed-for and terrifying like the perverse femininity it comes to stand for, in the dreams of the second Mrs de Winter, now living with Max in virtual exile abroad. More conventional both in its writing and its outlook than *Orlando*, *Rebecca* shares Woolf's love affair with the landed classes, a conservative romance with place and class that is also explicitly aligned with experiment and transgression in relation to femininity.

Radclyffe Hall's watershed lesbian novel, *The Well of Loneliness* appeared in 1928, the same year as *Orlando*. While most critics have highlighted Hall's representation of homosexuality, almost as fascinating is the author's depiction of normative femininity, at once harsher and more sentimental than any of the other writers we have been discussing. Like *Orlando*, *The Well of Loneliness* imagines the transformation of gender in terms of the landed English gentry, as Jaime Hovey has argued. Hall fantasises a privileged childhood in her creation of Morton Hall, the country seat in the Malvern Hills of Sir Philip and Lady Anna Gordon, and their daughter and only child, the novel's 'invert' protagonist, Stephen

Gordon. *The Well of Loneliness* focuses on the way in which biological females *don't* necessarily become women, tracing instead the path to maturity of a girl who identifies as a boy. Stephen becomes an adult who adopts a masculine style and is attracted to other women. In *The Well of Loneliness* femininity becomes a lost object of desire: something that Stephen can neither be nor have. Unachievable and elusive, the feminine becomes both overvalued and degraded, invested in things as well as people. Morton Hall is described in the opening sentences of the novel through a nostalgic evocation of the femininity of the past, 'like certain lovely women who, now old, belong to a bygone generation – women who in youth were passionate but seemly; difficult to win but when won, all-fulfilling' (Hall 1990 [1928]: 3). At first Anna Molloy, Stephen's mother, seems a present incarnation of such idealized femininity: 'lovely as only an Irish woman can be, having that in her bearing that betokened quiet pride, having that in her eyes that betokened great longing, having that in her body that betokened happy promise – the archetype of the very perfect woman, whom creating God had found good' (3) Sir Philip's overwhelming desire for a son and heir is frustrated when Anna bears a daughter; in his disappointment he persuades his wife to keep the male name they have agreed upon. But as the 'narrow-hipped, wide-shouldered' baby (5), turns into a tomboyish 'queer' child an 'almost grotesque' shyness develops between mother and daughter (7) , and Anna's attitude towards Stephen who so closely resembled her loved husband degenerates into 'antagonism', 'anger' and distaste (8).

Sir Philip is represented as both noble and tolerant, but as Anna imagines her child as 'a blemished, unworthy, maimed reproduction' of its father, the mother's narrow sympathies are exposed (8). Nobility in *The Well of Loneliness* is associated with the 'true' masculinity that Philip possesses; Stephen's yearning for nobility is an early sign of her masculine identification as she innocently tells the servants that '"I must be a boy, 'cause I feel exactly like one, I feel like young Nelson in the picture upstairs"' (13). Fantasies of male heroism are later merged with more romantic and intellectual ones as Stephen becomes the Byronic figure, suggested by her surname, class and choice of writing as a profession. Rejected by her beautiful mother, who tries to impose a superficial femininity of dress and decorum on her awkward child, Stephen desperately pursues the elusive feminine in a series of inappropriate love objects: a young female servant, a bored local housewife, Angela Crosby, and finally the love of her life, the Welsh orphan, Mary Llewellyn. From Anna through Mary, each of these conventionally feminine women ends in betraying her: her mother's bigotry, Angela's fear of her husband and her own social position, Mary's growing love for Stephen's old friend Martin – each of these proximate causes springs from the constellation of characteristics that make up a small-minded, shallow and inconstant femininity. *The Well of Loneliness* historicizes femininity as it tracks the changed opportunities for women in the incremental understanding of gender and its more perverse manifestations from Stephen's Edwardian childhood to the First World War and its aftermath. Yet there is another more static and ahistorical register in the novel by which so called 'normal' femininity is seen, through the longing and misogyny of unmet desire, as both hopelessly idealized and ethically wanting – expressing in the end a deformity of spirit as immovable as the biology that Hall believes is responsible for the existence of 'inverts'. The scientific theories that underpin Hall's concept of a 'third sex' – her novel is dedicated to 'Our three selves' – were drawn from the sexology of her time formulated by Havelock Ellis and Krafft-Ebing. However, her contradictory representation of traditional femininity draws on both popular prejudice and on a feminist-inspired revulsion at the narrative closure of female rebellion and independence in conventional marriage and motherhood. At the end of *Well of Loneliness* Stephen tricks Mary into abandoning her for Martin and a protected heterosexual life in Canada. Once Mary is narratively disposed of, Stephen's future can be invested in the noble defence of her 'kind'. And in this crusade her nobility and wide sympathies fully emerge as she champions not only female 'inverts' but male homosexuals as well, whom the novel represents as the bearers of the most degraded femininity of all, the simulated, grotesque femininity of gay men, with their 'shaking, white-skinned effeminate fingers' (505).

Of the English and Irish women writers we have been discussing, only Woolf was a self-described feminist. Indeed, only Woolf had radical or progressive views on issues other than gender: Hall had fascist leanings, du Maurier was a conservative, and Bowen, as her biographer Victoria Glendinning notes, 'moved further to the right as she got older' (Glendinning 1993: 231). Although the interwar period in Britain witnessed plenty of activism around women's rights from men and women who saw these as part of larger social and political agendas, in this generation of women writers the wish to challenge the norms of gender and to invent new forms of femininity were not necessarily aligned with liberal views on other issues. Nevertheless Bowen, Woolf, Hall and du Maurier have become part of a new literary canon of twentieth-century women writers whose fiction explored the century's new sense of gender, experimenting as much with the narrative forms through which it could be represented as with the limits of what one could say about it. Impatient with the constraints and pieties of both middle-class femininity and middle-class feminism, their fantasies of gender freedom or gender transgression as an identity that might be 'mad, bad and dangerous to know' become entangled in different ways with an image of aristocracy and its privileges rather than with that of a revolution from below.

RACE AND FEMININITY IN AFRICAN AMERICAN WRITING

Class and ethnicity were by no means the exclusive or local concerns of women from Britain or Ireland, but qualified and complicated in different ways all the new femininities invented and narrated by women in the Anglophone societies of the 1920s and 1930s, where women were newly enfranchised. Moreover, to see how some of the same issues about the role of sexual freedom in the rights and freedoms that women might now claim surface, albeit with a different history, when femininity is parsed through the grammars of race and class we can turn to African American women writers in the United States in the same decades. The growth of a Black middle class after the abolition of slavery, a class regarded by spokespersons like W.E.B. DuBois to be the agent of progress for all African Americans, placed a heavy responsibility on the morals and demeanour of its women. The myths created through slavery and racism about the promiscuous sexuality of African American women were to be refuted by the virtuous, educated and civic-minded mothers, wives and daughters of the black bourgeoisie, whose women leaders saw themselves as at once the shock troops and domestic stronghold of 'race' politics. Frances Ellen Watkins Harper's *Iola Leroy* (1987 [1892]) offered readers a heroine of just this sort.

In the interwar years, however, an altogether different kind of heroine begins somewhat hesitatingly to emerge, in fictions which rebel against the novel whose main ideological thrust was the advancement of the race or the femininity it championed. Janie Crawford, the protagonist of Zora Neale Hurston's *Their Eyes Were Watching God* (1936), comes from the rural poor, is thrice married, and is forced to kill her last and most loved husband, Tea Cake Woods. The sort of agency Janie wants and the femininity she inhabits have little to do with either upward mobility or the advance of the race, but are rather the pursuit of both passion and 'to find out about livin'' first hand (Hurston 1937: 183). Her second marriage to the store-owner, Joe Starks, leaves Janie excluded from both these possibilities. The novel's narrative voice-over and the vernacular exchanges of its characters allow anthropologist Hurston to raise Janie's quest for love and knowledge to the level of a 'folk' philosophy. Through the voices of the Southern poor in her short stories and non-fiction Hurston obliquely resists the middle-class terms through which both racial and gender aspirations might be channelled. Yet critic Cheryl Wall suggests that in *Their Eyes Were Watching God*, Hurston is arguing that the social values identified with white materialist society cannot be evaded, but were at work even in the most marginal communities of the South, personified not only in propertied men like Starks, but by the light-skinned restaurant proprietor, Mrs Turner, 'whose attempt to replicate the social hierarchy of the larger [white] society causes Janie and Tea Cake to revert to the stereotyped gender roles that society endorses' (Wall 1995: 191).

Wall's comment prompts the questions of where those stereotypes originated, and of which class within a minority culture adopted and endorsed them. Were the repressive social and sexual standards of the Black middle class that Deborah McDowell argues continued to inhibit the work of most African American women writers in the interwar years, especially in their representation of black female sexuality, simply a replication of nineteenth-century white standards of 'pure womanhood'? Even more than in the British texts of the 1920s and 1930s female sexuality is the key to the revision of femininity in African American women's writing. Because of the long history and durability of 'social and literary myths . . . about black women's libidinousness' reaching back to slavery, but more virulent perhaps after its abolition, McDowell explains that 'even into the Freudian 1920's, the Jazz Age of sexual abandon and "free love" – when female sexuality, in general, was acknowledged and commercialized in the advertising, beauty, and fashion industries – black women's novels preserve their reticence about sexuality', leaving its open expression to 'black female blues singers' who sang about its pleasures and dangers in the vernacular speech of the poor (McDowell 1986: xiii). Class difference fractures the kind of femininity that could be dreamed of and written about in this period. The sexual politics of black expression surfaced as a contested issue in the aesthetic debates among black artists and intellectuals in the 'Harlem Renaissance'. It dictated the reserve, McDowell argues, that pervades the work of one of the most experimental and compelling writers of the period, Nella Larsen, whose two memorable novels, *Quicksand* (1928) and *Passing* (1929) directly and tragically confront the contradictions and constraints of black bourgeois femininity. The restless young heroine of *Quicksand*, Helga Crane, leaves her teaching job at a black southern school, Naxos (Saxon spelt backward) which 'was now a show place . . . exemplification of the white man's magnanimity' (Larsen 1986: 4). The school 'tolerated no innovations, no individualisms' and 'Enthusiasm, spontaneity, if not actually suppressed, were at least openly regretted as unladylike or ungentlemanly qualities' (4), so that Helga had come to hate 'the trivial hypocrisies and careless cruelties' which were 'a part of the Naxos policy of uplift' (5). In addition Helga's lack of connections to the leading families of Negro society, which was, Larsen tells us, 'as complicated and as rigid in its ramifications as the highest strata of white society', meant that her individuality had to be suppressed (8). In gendered terms the Naxos ethos rewards 'ladyness' (12), and when Helga resigns, the head tries to flatter her by saying that she is a 'lady' who brings 'dignity and breeding' to the school; it gives Helga some satisfaction to tell him that 'My father was a gambler who deserted my mother, a white immigrant' (21).

Helga's search for less constricted gender identity and a wider field for her inchoate ambitions, which Larsen characterizes as a finely tuned aesthetic sense, takes her first to New York where she becomes part of a sophisticated and monied black society light years removed from the provincial Naxos, and later to Europe where she moves with her white Aunt and Uncle in white society. None of these contexts gives her enduring satisfactions, but are instead a series of dead ends in which she feels trapped by the enclosing walls of societies built, in different ways, on racial exclusion; in Europe she escapes the pretensions of the black bourgeoisie for one that is freer but in which she is regarded as an exotic commodity. And Helga herself is constantly censoring what she believes is illicit and regressive in her own sensuous desires, associating them with African primitivism – 'the jungle'. Larsen cannot resolve the dilemma she has set for Helga or her narrative; the novel's hardly bearable or credible conclusion finds Helga back in a Southern small town, married to a black preacher, Reverend Pleasant Green, whom she loathes, condemned to a life of endless childbearing. McDowell argues that the unsettling and downbeat ending of Larsen's novel, in which the turn to conventional marriage is a form of living death, is Larsen's response to the 'contradictory impulses' that inspired *Quicksand.* 'Larsen wanted to tell the story of the black woman with sexual desires, but was constrained by a competing desire to establish black women as respectable in black middle-class terms', a conflict that has 'strangling effects . . . both on her characters and on her narratives' (McDowell 1986: xvi).

Larsen's fiction suggests how closely meshed the determinants of race and class are in the making of gendered subjectivity, as well as just how misleading it can be to make too strong a distinction between the categories of gender and sexuality when thinking through the representation of femininity. In *Orlando, Rebecca* and *The Well of Loneliness,* racial difference acts as a subtheme or motif in more overtly class-bound discussions of gender. Whiteness, as a privileged form of gendered identity, is subliminally present as a kind of consolation prize for the trials of being a woman. But Larsen, drawing on and revising the literary figure of the 'tragic mulatto', the woman of mixed race who had been long a favoured figure of racialized femininity deployed by both white and black writers, makes the raced element of femininity and its discontents central to her texts and to her light-skinned protagonists, Helga Crane and Clare Kendry of *Passing,* each of whom is the product of a cross-racial liaison. As Cheryl Wall points out, Larsen's use of the mulatto subverts 'the convention consistently. . . . They are neither noble nor long-suffering; their plights are not used to symbolize the oppression of blacks, the irrationality of prejudice, or the absurdity of concepts of race generally' (Wall 1995: 89). Instead, Wall argues, they focus on the psychological effects of 'racism and sexism' which make 'self-definition' impossible for black women (89).

Passing takes on, as well, the impossible attraction between women, highlighting another common element of women's writing about women in this period: femininity, especially highly sexed, hyper-femininity, less as a lure and danger to men than as the site of desire between women. In this novel Larsen has taken the conflict between respectability and desire that destroyed Helga Crane and split it into two characters, girlhood friends drawn to each other in mid-life. Irene Redfield is a repressed, respectable Harlem doctor's wife, whose 'passing' for white is limited to an occasional day out at a posh department store; here, one day, she re-encounters the beautiful Clare Kendry who has married a bullying white businessman, and concealed her racial origin, but risks everything by renewing her friendship with Irene and the black middle-class cultural milieu to which she belongs. As Deborah McDowell points out, the novel, by eroticizing Clare's exotic beauty – her 'tempting mouth', and her seductive ways, the 'caress' of her gaze – as seen through the fascinated and fearful eyes of Irene, more than hints at their mutual attraction (McDowell 1986: xxvii). The surreal denouement of the novel, when Clare, her racial identity suddenly revealed to her racist husband, falls or is pushed to her death from a Harlem balcony, suggests the impossibility not only of black female identity but of same sex desire.

Feminist theorist Judith Butler's analysis of Larsen's novel, 'Passing, Queering', argues that the social and psychological readings of *Passing* ought not to be seen as in conflict; she suggests that race (whiteness as much as blackness) is constituent to the psychic terms of sexual difference. Butler pushes this argument one crucial theoretical step further, insisting that there is no 'relationship called "sexual difference" that is itself unmarked by race' (Butler 1993: 181). 'What becomes psychically repressed in *Passing* is linked to the specificity of the social constraints on black women's sexuality that inform Larsen's text' (179). These recent analyses of Larsen's work have quite properly seen her bold if ambivalent attempt to make the repression of black female sexuality, rather than its exploitation, the key problem and the potential tragedy of the women in her texts. Hazel Carby argues that Larsen's exposure of the contradictions involved in the representation of Helga Crane 'as a sexual being', even if they are ones she cannot resolve, makes Helga 'the first truly sexual black female protagonist' in African American fiction (Carby 1987: 174). If we read women writers from the interwar years right across the racial and cultural divide, we can see that sexual freedom, with its pleasures and dangers, is for all of them in a variety of ways, the linchpin of their criticism of middle-class femininity, and by implication the middle-class campaign for women's rights of which they were now the supposed beneficiaries. Virginia Woolf herself embodies those tensions and contradictions when, in 1929, she predicted happily that these new civic freedoms would liberate women into writing fiction that would involve 'a turn towards the impersonal' which would make 'her novels . . . more critical of society, and less analytical of individual lives'. She would write novels which would 'deal with social evils and remedies. Their men and women will not be observed wholly in relation to each other emotionally, but as they cohere and clash in groups and classes and races' (Woolf 1979: 50–1). She is not the only writer to be dissatisfied with the imaginative ghetto of the 'personal' – in *The Last September*, Lois rejects the idea of being a writer as 'so embarrassing. . . . Even things like – like elephants get so personal' (Bowen 1998: 98). Woolf, who had argued elsewhere that women in the twentieth century should be able to write 'the truth of the body', is perhaps defending women writers against the old accusation that all their work would be narrowly personal and subjective and that femininity rendered women constitutionally and culturally incapable of a wider vision. The understanding that sexuality as well as gender were a part of the politics of 'groups, classes', races and nations was an idea taking shape but not fully articulated in the interwar years. Woolf's conservative defence reflects how hard it was to resist the binary definitions of gender which made the 'personal' and the 'emotional', which we might translate as sexuality and the psychic, part of a degraded femininity, rather than crucial issues for the societies in which, as she rightly remarks, women would now be able to act for themselves and 'not merely influence the acts of others' (Woolf 1979: 50).

In view of the way in which these fictions by women highlight sexuality, depicted in terms of race and class rather than as outside their categorical jurisdictions, as a centrally unresolved issue *within* the reorientation brought about by the new freedoms of postwar society, one might see Freud's conclusion in 'Femininity' in a slightly different light. When he suggests that understanding sexuality and its psychic effects 'goes very far', if not far enough, towards resolving the 'riddle' of femininity', he may be no more, although no less, than at one with the *Zeitgeist* he helped to create.

MASCULINE IDENTIFICATION: FEMININITY'S DISAPPEARING ACT

In thinking beyond femininity in its past and present incarnations, both theorists and imaginative writers have invented narratives in which feminine abjection can be transformed, displaced or otherwise evaded. One strategy, as we have seen, is to look to the past: when Brontë chooses to have the child Jane Eyre align her resistant and angry self with 'any other rebel slave', she does so in the years *after* the abolition of colonial slavery in British colonies (Brontë 1987: 9). Similarly, the aristocratic identifications in Woolf, Bowen and Hall are nostalgic ones – a displacement into the past of privilege. Another strategy exploits the fantasies of upward mobility so endemic to capitalist societies. In mass-market fiction – in Harlequin or Mills and Boon romance and the blockbusters and bodice-rippers which target women readers – a favoured move has been to alleviate the restrictions of gender by conferring on women status and money rather than democratically extended rights and opportunities. The avant-garde as well as the popular has been keen to displace the narrative of female degradation and melancholia. French feminist theory and fiction of the 1960s and 1970s that called itself 'écriture feminine' was committed to transforming gender, and what was written about it, by celebrating as well as changing femininity. We have looked at Wittig's linguistic and narrative experiments in the previous chapter. She is one of many feminists from the late 1960s onwards who chose to take up modernist strategies or who turned to utopian and science fiction to find a style or genre which would allow them to bypass the seeming inevitability not just of gender binaries but of femininity itself as a trajectory for little girls, with an identity called 'woman' as its necessary outcome.

Yet in literature as in life, as Snitow's interlocutor suggests, resistance to a particular social narrative of gender may take the form of the fantasy of being a man, although it is always a fantasy with problems and limits, a fantasy that, whether simply imagined or acted out tends simultaneously to undermine and to confirm gendered identity. The history of female cross-dressing is well documented, and its place in western social practice and imagination has been much analysed of late. *Orlando*, of course, is a playful incarnation of this fantasy but Woolf cleverly keeps the mechanism which alters Orlando's gender safely in the control of the author rather than her protagonist; similarly Radclyffe Hall makes the fantasy itself a narrative dead end for Stephen Gordon who must turn to theories of a 'third sex' to advance the human rights of homosexuals. Hall's fictional crusade has become reality; as trans-gendered and transexual humans acquire more rights in western democracies, so it becomes more possible for imagined gender to be lived out.

In the first half century of psychoanalysis the persistence of women's identification with masculinity into adult life – her 'masculinity complex' – was a favoured topic for analysis; to understand the psychic process whereby adult women fail to relinquish such 'infantile identification' – the masculine stage – was thought a route to understanding female homosexuality. In 1929, the psychoanalyst Joan Riviere published a fascinating essay on the meaning of so-called masculine identification in otherwise 'feminine' women. 'Womanliness as a Masquerade' highlighted the performative status of femininity. Riviere foregrounds just those groups of professional women who were emerging in the period, women who, in her view:

> seem to fulfil every criterion of complete feminine development. They are excellent wives and mothers, capable housewives; they maintain social life and assist culture; they have no lack of feminine interests, e.g. in their personal appearance, and when called upon they can still find time to play the part of devoted and disinterested mother-substitutes among a wide circle of relatives and friends.
>
> (Riviere 1986: 36)

For Riviere, who saw the social categories of gender in relatively conservative terms, the fact that these women 'fulfil the duties of their profession at least as well as the average man' makes them a 'puzzle' to classify psychologically (36). Her leading 'case study' involves 'a woman of this kind . . . engaged in work of a propagandist nature, which consisted principally in speaking and writing' who suffered extreme anxiety after every successful performance, worried whether she had done 'anything inappropriate' and in desperate need of reassurance, both about the competence of her performance and her sexual attraction, from men who were 'unmistakable father figures' (36). Yet in unravelling this and other similar cases, Riviere comes to a surprising and radical conclusion. She does not argue, as she might, that the supposed masculine activities of such women are cross-gender 'performances' (although the logic of her analysis implies that they are), but rather that femininity – womanliness – is itself a 'masquerade', and one, moreover, that many woman adopt as a defence against the extreme anxiety produced by masculine identification. While Riviere roots her analysis in contemporary psychoanalytic debates about the psychic stages of infancy and early childhood, her exploration leads her to ask a much broader question in her conclusion: 'what is the essential nature of fully developed femininity?' (43). As if she herself must propitiate the gods of gender whose special task it is to keep masculinity and femininity in place as binary terms, she seems through this question to draw back from her own startling answer that no such 'essential nature' exists.

Cross-gendered fantasy in general must be viewed as a crucial part of imaginative life. Certainly it is the *sine qua non* of the creative process, and especially of fiction and drama, for what novelist or dramatist could survive without it? However, there is a more disturbing logic within certain feminist narratives that moves inexorably from a critique of the feminine as it is expressed in particular cultures and social groups, to an identification with and/ or an idealization of the masculine, as if femininity were a kind of disappointing daughter to be discarded for a more favoured son. In these narratives the problems and burdens of femininity are magically resolved through a kind of sleight of hand in which a 'woman' becomes 'more like a man', psychologically and socially, and is thereby positioned in a brave new world where the privileges and priorities of gender inequality have disappeared. This turn towards masculinity as a refuge from an embattled and undervalued femininity seems, at one level, perfectly rational, but at another it only intensifies the 'puzzle' about the nature of femininity and feminism. It points to feminism's simultaneous censure and envy of the masculine as well as its own latent misogyny – or at the very least its suspicion that there is something irremediably wrong, not only with the universal preference that human cultures give to men, but with female subjectivity itself. In a striking number of feminist texts from Mary Wollstonecraft's *A Vindication of the Rights of Woman* to the feminist science fictions that have been invented from the 1970s onwards, there are points where the lady seems to vanish and her place is taken by virtual masculinity. In order to see what is at stake when femininity performs this kind of disappearing act we need to look more closely at how gender and its effects are represented in such texts.

In *The Left Hand of Darkness*, Ursula K. LeGuin's 1969 novel about a planet of androgynes, a female anthropologist from a future federation of ordinary, two-sexed human worlds reflects on the liberating but frightening possibilities of a society without fixed gender. On Gethen, she muses, there is 'no myth of Oedipus', 'no unconsenting sex', 'no division of humanity into strong and weak halves'. Unique among the varieties of mankind that people the known universe, Gethen is a place where 'the whole tendency to dualism that pervades human thinking may be found to be lessened or changed' (LeGuin 1977: 69). Yet even for LeGuin's sympathetic social scientist, trained as she is to encounter and accept new ways of being, the ontological shift that signals the collapse of dualism's old certainties about sexual difference registers as shocking and terrifying. Its abandonment threatens the categories of thinking itself, as well as those of selfhood. It challenges the very ground on which ethics are based. Convention is all, even if it is a convention of radical inequality, so that for a species whose sense of self has been fashioned from and through the deformations of gender to be suddenly 'respected and judged only as a human being . . . is an appalling experience' (70).

Daughter of the anthropologists Alfred Louis and Theodora Kroeber, LeGuin often conceives her science fictions as didactic ethnographies. Her alien worlds and peoples combine elements of actual and imaginary human cultures, while her plots are parables of humanity's worst excesses and best impulses. Written in the first years of the second wave of the women's movement in North America and Western Europe, *The Left Hand of Darkness* echoes a utopian desire at least as old as the feminism that inspired it, evoking (if never citing) Mary Wollstonecraft's 'wild wish . . . to see the distinction of sex confounded in society, unless where love animates the behaviour' (Wollstonecraft 1988: 57). On Gethen, Wollstonecraft's wish is achieved in part by effacing one of the significant differences between the sexual lives of animals and humans: LeGuin's androgynes, like earth's animal species, are restricted to brief and exclusive periods of desire and sexual activity. In this recurring active phase sexual difference asserts itself as an arbitrary effect of each discrete periodic encounter. Whether one will become a 'man' or a 'woman' in any given pairing is outside the willed control of the individual or the couple, but the result is always a heterosexual union. So while LeGuin keeps a two sexed model in play, she also relegates it to a restricted space in Gethenian life; her androgynes are only properly men or women when 'animated by love'. In their fertile years these perfectly hermaphrodite beings both bear children and father them so that everyone is equally liable to be 'tied down to childbearing'. The psychic and social divisions of labour, which LeGuin sees as more or less inevitable in a world where only one sex reproduces, are evaded, and the happy result is that 'Anyone can turn his hand to anything' (LeGuin 1977: 69).

No more or less innocent than Freud's division of labour into those who can think gender and those who only display it, LeGuin's provocative use of the generic masculine for her androgyne species points to a familiar paradox at the heart of her egalitarian vision of an undivided human subject – the hate–love relationship that women have for most types of femininity as they are embodied and lived in any given historical moment. Androgyny, what Francette Pacteau has called 'the impossible referent', is less a solution to the revulsion than a clarification of its problem. Indeed her essay takes its title from *The Left Hand of Darkness*, citing the human male, Genly Ai, when he says of his Gethenian friend that 'it was impossible to think of him as a woman . . . and yet whenever I thought of him as a man I felt a sense of falseness, of imposture' (LeGuin 1977:16).

An incomplete or simulated masculinity has often been preferred to the impossible feminine. Late eighteenth-century feminism framed its distaste for femininity as an excess of desire *for* femininity; Wollstonecraft puts it baldly, even brutally, in *A Vindication*: 'This desire of being always women, is the very consciousness that degrades the sex' (Wollstonecraft 1988: 99). 'Women' or 'the sex' was the negative site of gender in the eighteenth century; femininity often measured the distance or decline from the human ideal. Early feminists, launching their critique both at the every day androcentrism of bourgeois society and at the theorized misogyny of progressive social philosophers such as Rousseau, shared an uncomfortable common ground with their opponents in their dislike of actually existing femininity. But while Rousseau believed that the feminine was innate, and recommended restraint as the only cure for its inevitable excesses, Wollstonecraft argued that it was cultural, and therefore open to reform. Rejecting biological determinism, and its accompanying fatalism about the future of sexual difference, she believed that women could and should transform their 'degraded' consciousness through exercising their latent rationality or 'understanding'. It 'should be the first object of laudable ambition . . . to obtain a character as a human being, regardless of the distinction of sex', wrote Wollstonecraft, but her 'human being' is remarkably close to an eighteenth-century ideal of masculinity (Wollstonecraft 1988: 9–10). It sometimes seems that the scenario of women's slow but steady emergence from their subaltern status rests not only on the assumption that women are made not born, but on a model of regendered humanity that owes more to imagined masculinity than to any other. Now and then *The Left Hand of Darkness* reminds the reader, almost as an afterthought, that Gethenians are women as well as men, but for most of the time masculinity is imaginatively as well as grammatically the default mode of subjectivity on Gethen.

When Genly Ai, the male dimorphic emissary to Gethen, is asked by his androgyne friend Therem Harth what women are like, he comments first on what they are less likely to be – mathematicians, great musicians – before his capacity to describe them falters and then fails: "'I can't tell you what women are like. . . . In a sense women are more alien to me than you are'" (LeGuin 1977: 160). In this way LeGuin reads back to us the problem of gender difference at its most extreme, for in Genly's failure to describe femininity we can also perceive a failure or fault line in LeGuin's profoundly humanist project, for its success rests on the perception of similarity – on human commonality and the sense of community and affiliation that should, but often does not, flow from this basic connection. Underneath Ai's rueful afterthought that 'You and I share one sex, at least' (160) lies the sense of something unspeakable and negative in the feminine, and something noble and expressible in the masculine, a difference as 'impossible' as the androgyny that pretends to change it.

Women's imaginative evocation of masculinity as a scene for idealized human relationships, both social and erotic, in the late twentieth century has taken some strange and wonderful forms. Cultural critic Constance Penley writes about a subgroup of fanzine culture around the US TV series *Star Trek* which imagines in stories, drawing and videos drawn from the actual programmes, an explicit sexual romance between Captain James T. Kirk of the USS *Enterprise* and his Vulcan first officer, Mr Spock. The K/S zine is one of a number of 'slash' fanzine's which publish stories that eroticize male duos from television series. Penley suggests that the K/S narratives '"retool"' existing masculinity, making it more 'sensitive and nurturing' than that which exists around them, but she also argues that the 'slash characters have to be male' because:

> the fans do indeed reject the female body as a terrain of fantasy or utopian thinking, but the female body they are rejecting is the body of the woman as it has been constituted in this culture: a body that is a legal, moral and religious battleground; a body seen as murderously dangerous to the foetus it may house; a body held to painfully higher standards of beauty than the male body.
>
> (Penley 1992: 498)

The K/Sers, most of whom are self-described straight women, do not and will not call themselves feminists, but their transgressive reworking of the emotional and sexual possibilities of what is already an avowedly humanist series, if it stops short of a worked out political critique of either femininity or feminism, does seek to ask the same question that LeGuin's novel poses. What is the future of femininity and of humans, if men are the new women? The utopian element of such writing cannot be easily pinned down as a naive escape from or denial of femininity and its discontents, or conversely, flagged as a simple radical revision of it. Like LeGuin's androgyne planet, its very existence troubles a more settled commonsense humanism that holds out hope for a better deal for gender in all its manifestations.

How well and how much can men or women understand or imagine their own or the other sex? Are the limits of such understanding, if limits there are, a reason for humanist despair? In making her male protagonist unable to define what 'women are like' LeGuin both reproduces and criticizes Sigmund Freud's conclusion to 'Femininity', where he concedes with deceptive candour that his 'incomplete and fragmentary' discussion 'does not always sound friendly'. Freud adds that of course he has only 'been describing women in so far as their nature is determined by their sexual function' and although 'that influence extends very far; we do not overlook the fact that an individual woman may be a human being in other respects as well.' Freud 1973: 169). Both the vagueness of 'other respects' and the conditional tense of 'may be a human being' underline how provisional and problematic a woman's identity as a 'human being' might be.

The Left Hand of Darkness imagines a cross-species love between Gethenian and human that cannot be consummated, a love that is composed, like that between men and women, and like that of women for their femininity, of attraction and repulsion. While Gethenians are a kind of material realization of Freud's universal notion of bisexuality, their embodiment of that acknowledgement, of the fact that difference is in great part a fiction, makes them, for humans, figures of taboo, both noble and untouchable.

POST-HUMAN(IST) FEMININITY?

A 1999 cover of the *New Yorker* magazine, in an issue devoted to 'Style' at the millennium, depicts a robot undergoing what seems to be a complete servicing (Roberts 1999). A mechanical claw tightens a loose screw in its head while others apply lipstick to its mouth and matching polish to its incongruous long nails. Yet another attachment brushes the robot's hair. 'It' is a 'she', and 'she' is made to look apprehensive rather than cosseted by all this attention, as well she may. An equation is being made between style, which has increasingly become an ambivalent shorthand for many aspects of modern societies, from politics to computers, and femininity. The cartoon depicts femininity as style only: the body and its differences are dispensable. A minimal visual code, and a bit of affect – bewildered and a bit frightened will do – can, the artist implies, make a woman of anything. The image suggests that these superficial adornments are all that is left of and for femininity at the end of the twentieth century. Does it also imply that the work of feminism and of modernity in denaturalizing the body has gone a tad too far – or not far enough? The robot's femininity, like the Cheshire Cat's smile in Lewis Carroll's *Alice in Wonderland*, lingers on uncannily, as both accessory and affect, commerce and sensibility, while the living 'body' of femininity has disappeared.

African-American legal theorist and essayist Patricia Williams puts such questions in the context of the 'grotesque' representations of gender in the United States, which are tied, she argues, to the fetishization of racial embodiment. Through the language of disembodied little sounds she describes listening to her mother as she 'does her face and hair':

> I can hear the anxiety of her preparations: the creaking of the floorboards as she stands closer then farther from the mirror;

the lifting and replacing of infinite bottles and jars on the shelves; the click of her closing a compact of blush; the running of water over her hairbrush; an anonymous fidgety frequency of sounds. She is a constancy of small motions, clatters, soft rattles and bumps.

(Williams 1991: 196)

Performing the same ritual herself, Williams (rather like the *New Yorker* cartoon) realizes that when 'I am fully-dressed, my face is hung with contradictions; I try not to wear all my contradictions at the same time. I pick and choose among them' (ibid.: 196). Her ironic reflection on the meaning of 'choice' echoes the mixed message of the *New Yorker* cover.

Can the machine become a labour-saving fantasy for the feminist imagination, taking over the jobs that marked femininity as too embodied but not quite human enough? In the utopian feminist writings of the 1970s technology was positively appropriated as a way of releasing women from reproduction: Marge Piercy's novel *Woman on the Edge of Time* (1976) pursued the analysis of Shulamith Firestone's *The Dialectic of Sex* (1979 [1970]) by making gestation and childbirth an out-of-body experience, and 'mothering' a task shared between men and women. The dystopian future, in which women are valued only for their capacity to reproduce, is sketched out in Margaret Atwood's bleak fiction, *The Handmaid's Tale* (1986). In a counter-move, certain feminist thinkers have tried to build a new version of ethics on the psychic and social relations that they believe flow from women's role in child rearing, if not childbirth. The media debate about the uses of increasingly sophisticated reproductive technologies erupts into the public domain with each new 'discovery', and is mirrored by profound disagreements within feminism about the benefits of such technology. At the same time, the pro-natalist, anti-abortionist and often Fundamentalist opinion in the United States, by no means a male-only stronghold, has helped to carry laws which protect the foetus to the extent of criminalizing the pregnant mother-to-be who drinks or smokes, thus disaggregating the rights and identities of mother and unborn child in novel and frightening ways, and giving a new twist to a long tradition of contradictory representations of motherhood as both idealized and pathologizied. Technology has altered not just the fact of motherhood, but also profoundly affected its representation as an aspect of gender. The spread of birth control and the legalization of abortion in the 1970s seemed to offer more autonomy to women in every aspect of their lives, not simply in respect of sexuality and reproduction, and thus to shift the relations of power between men and women. But the enhanced possibility of 'choice', through the availability of contraception, and to a lesser extent abortion, has provided, as an ironic corollary, a further instrument of state control of poor mothers, who may have their benefits withdrawn if they have additional children while receiving state support. It is possible that, paradoxically, maternal femininity has become both more liberated and more regulated.

In a 'A Cyborg Manifesto' feminist theorist Donna Haraway pursues the metaphor of the 'cyborg', that 'hybrid of machine and organism', as a way of 'imagining a world without gender', one which both short-circuits and supersedes unresolved and perhaps unresolvable debates about origins and differences, nature and culture (Haraway 1991: 149–50). 'Cyborg imagery', Haraway suggested hopefully in the mid-1980s, was 'a way out of the maze of dualisms' in which gender, and feminism too, had become enmeshed and imprisoned (ibid.: 181). Haraway's essay turns on its use of irony and contradiction; it was conceived in a 'postmodernist, non-naturalist mode and in the utopian tradition' (150) and set its face determinedly against the recreation within feminism of a new 'organicism', for gender or for femininity, against any theory which essentializes gender by turning to myths of goddesses or of fecundity. If feminism must have a myth, Haraway suggested, it has to be one which incorporates its own critique of identity, it must embody the components of modernity it might make use of, including technology, and it should emphasize women – and feminism's – radical heterogeneity. Haraway's model is one which tries to make incommensurable elements connect: she envisages a working alliance that can live with the discomfort and difficulty that we have suggested is the condition of femininity, indeed of gender.

Haraway herself has been criticized for suggesting that 'women of colour' – a politically crafted category that comprises different ethnic and diasporic groups in political alliance – can be imagined as one type of 'cyborg'. For those subjects still struggling to be regarded as 'human' by states and societies, the anti-human, post-gendered metaphor may not be as liberating as it looks. Nevertheless, blurring the boundaries between the human and its others has remained a tempting strategy for what Haraway evocatively calls 'the imagi-native apprehension, of oppression, and so of possibility' (149). When Patricia Williams imagines a world without racism or gender hierarchy, she crosses over into an animal world as fabulous as Haraway's cyborgs, a world, rather like the femininity she inhabits, 'ambiguously natural and crafted' (Haraway 1991: 149). Williams's fantasy landscape is arctic; it is significantly without sound or affect: a world of polar bears, of 'white wind', 'shadowed amnesia; the absence of being . . . cool fragments of white-fur invisibility. Solid, black-gummed, intent, observant' (Williams 1991: 236). Her polar bears are the poetic expression of creative paradox, not so much a dream beyond the reach of the brutal ideologies of gender or colour, as its necessary correlative: a country at once familiar and alien, on whose strangely silent shores one can pause to regroup and reconsider the 'complexity of messages implied in our being' (236).

2

MASCULINITIES

We begin this chapter in what has long been thought of as a quintessentially male arena: the battlefield. Towards the close of *The Storm of Steel* (1929), the extraordinary memoir of his experiences as an officer in the First World War, the German writer Ernst Jünger recounts the story of how he escaped being captured, shooting enemy soldiers as he ran, even though his own body was riddled with bullets. Narrated with the surgical precision that was to become his trademark as a novelist – 'continuous loss of blood gave me the lightness and airiness of intoxication' he notes as he describes dodging and then returning enemy fire – Jünger's recollections come to a halt in a military hospital where the tone of his writing abruptly and rather unpredictably changes (Jünger 1929 [1920]: 312). Declaring himself to be 'no misogynist', the author cannot help but confess that:

> I was always irritated by the presence of women every time that the fate of battle threw me into the bed of a hospital ward. One sank, after the manly and purposeful activities of the war, into a vague atmosphere of warmth.

Only the 'clear objectivity of the Catholic nursing sisterhoods' offers an ambience that is at all 'congenial to soldiering', a blessed relief from the usual oppressively maternal regime (314).

To be sure, women do have their charms. Earlier in the narrative, when a 'friendly' seventeen-year-old, alone in her cottage, serves him a peasant supper Jünger is immediately struck by the 'ease of manner that one finds so often in France among quite simple girls' (66). For a moment he almost seems to forget that he is a member of an army of occupation and that he is enjoying his enemy's hospitality. But in the rather less idyllic setting of the military hospital a line must be drawn in the sand that will keep femininity at bay, despite the fact that these nurses are enlisted Germans sent to provide him with the care he so desperately needs. It is as if the tenderness of women might somehow further corrode the soldier's armoured psyche, already put at risk by his physical injuries. From the indignities of the hospital bed it seems impossible to recover the sense of gallant condescension that had once allowed him to find the young French woman so enchanting, so unthreatening.

The ferocious splitting of the nurses into the compassionate and the dispassionate, and the demand for a carefully distanced, rigorously unemotional system of care, speaks volumes about the precarious nature of Jünger's male ideal. His memoirs show masculinity at a historic turning point, a moment when ideas about what it meant to be a man were under maximum pressure from mass military mobilization and new, more deadly technologies of warfare. Underpinning the descriptions of manoeuvres and scenes of combat in *The Storm of Steel* is an account of Jünger's constant struggle to secure his sense of value as a man in the midst of the most appalling conditions, an account that lays bare the fragility of masculinity, its hopes and its weaknesses. Jünger learns to measure his tour of duty by a pitiless military code that is both intensely patriotic – the book closes with the words 'Germany lives and Germany shall never go under!' – and thoroughly preoccupied with upholding one's honour in front of the men from the lower ranks whose composure quickly slips away as soon as privation and danger strike (319).

Masculinity for Jünger requires careful definition, a discriminating eye. It may be rooted in social class, but class is a matter of birth and breeding, of what one is, not of what one achieves: its highest good is the nation, yet some nations, including his own as well as France, are prone to 'excessive national feeling', falling into vulgar and demeaning posturing, and failing to give the enemy his due (52). Women are no less of a problem, causing soldiers to forget themselves and thereby undermining true military decorum. When the men fraternize too closely with the civilian population they are liable to soften, to neglect their duties. Recalling one such episode in the village of Fresnoy-le-Grand, Jünger remembers 'the sounds of carnival in every billet' and coyly observes that 'Venus deprived Mars of many servants' before the 'old Prussian discipline' was restored (119).

Of course, Jünger's larger purpose is to commemorate the dead and to remind his readers why his comrades died. For once we cease to understand what it means for a man willingly to die for his country the whole idea of the Fatherland becomes meaningless: it too will have died. But, on another level, Jünger is defending what he regards as a model form of masculinity, one that is deserving of authority and respect, despite the terrible loss of life in which it is implicated. In a sense, *The Storm of Steel* seeks to make that loss intelligible through a direct appeal to a virtuous and selfless code, the ethic of the true warrior. In cultivating a militaristic sensibility, Jünger draws upon the full resources of German literary culture, quoting Nietzsche, Goethe and Schiller in the grand manner and pitting the 'manlier' Schiller against the decadent French sentiments of Stendhal. Jünger thus seeks to occupy the moral and cultural high ground, to ennoble his fellow officers even in – perhaps especially in – defeat.

Jünger's writing helps us to see some of the intensive cultural work that goes into securing masculinity and why so much seems to ride upon what men take themselves to be. But if Jünger's project of masculine regeneration is simply one attempt among many to shore up contemporary manhood, to restore it to its rightful place within the modern nation state (and restore the nation to its proper standing in the world), how does it relate to those gentler or less abrasive versions of masculinity with which it has been, at best, in competition, at worst, locked in a life and death struggle? To put this question in perspective we need to turn to a cultural history of masculinities.

'THE MANLY IDEAL'

Histories of this kind are still too new to be wholly uncontroversial, but a useful starting point is George Mosse's synoptic study of masculinity and modernity *The Image of Man* (1996), one of the last works written by a pioneer in the field. Mosse presents a broad brush survey that charts the rise and gradual erosion of what he variously calls 'the dominant masculine stereotype', 'normative masculinity', or, more simply, 'the manly ideal', a highly charged bundle of ideas that he traces back to the late eighteenth century. At the centre of this ideal lay a renewed emphasis upon the perfectibility of the male body, which became an outward sign of a man's moral superiority and inner strength of character. The body was to be a locus of self-discipline and restraint, able so to concentrate its energies that any obstacle could be surmounted, any hint of emotional weakness could be held in check.

This masculine ideal was intimately connected to the growth of a commercial and industrial bourgeoisie throughout Western Europe but, far from being a wishful self-portrait of one particular social class, it was a complex amalgam of beliefs and practices drawn from many sources, some old, some new. One key element was the eighteenth-century revival of interest in the ancient Greek ideal of male beauty associated with the writings of the archaeologist and art historian Johann Joachim Winckelmann (1717–68) who promoted the model of the young Greek athlete as the embodiment of what he called 'noble simplicity and quiet grandeur' (quoted in Mosse 1996: 29). Winckelmann's striking phrase brings out not only the fusion of the moral and the visual that was so important to the manly ideal, but the carefully qualified sense of dignity and pomp conveyed here also suggests its political potential as an inspirational image that might be taken to symbolize the nation, alongside the national anthem and the national flag. Among those deeply indebted to Winckelmann's work was the republican artist Jacques Louis David (1748–1825) whose neo-classical canvasses depicted the French revolutionaries as 'Greeks and Romans re-born', men whose stirring deeds were 'just as worthy of the painter's attention as the episodes of Greek and Roman history' (Gombrich 1978: 382).

Winckelmann's concept of beauty, which involved his praising the qualities of 'balance, proportion, and moderation', was sometimes criticized as forbiddingly abstract, too removed from real life (Mosse 1996: 33). But it did offer a kind of standard that ordinary bourgeois citizens might try to emulate, implying that the male body could be purified or purged of its imperfections. There was of course a long tradition of thought which claimed that an individual's moral well-being depended upon his physical fitness – we find this idea in *Émile* (1762), Jean-Jacques Rousseau's influential treatise on education, for example – and the early years of the nineteenth century saw the spread of popular gymnastics, particularly in Prussia where regimes of vigorous exercise were seen as a means of achieving German unity. According to Friedrich Ludwig Jahn's 1816 handbook *Deutsche Turnkunst* ('German Gymnastics') the aim of these disciplined exertions was to produce men that were 'chaste, pure, capable, fearless, truthful and ready to bear arms' (quoted in Mosse 1996: 43).

This ideal of masculinity therefore requires intense effort: a man must struggle against himself, even conceiving of his own body as a sort of enemy, and also against others. The differences between men and women had to be sharply emphasized and feminine traits had to be kept firmly in their proper place: in men they were a sign of weakness. Mosse argues that the manly ideal was partly defined by what it excluded, those unsightly features and pathological behaviours that indicated everything an authentic masculinity was not supposed to be. More than mere bad examples to be shunned and avoided at all costs, these negative images took the form of dangerous 'countertypes' that were thought to pose a real threat to the healthy body and ought therefore to be vigorously resisted. These ranged from cultural outsiders like the Jews or gypsies to those in the grip of practices that seemed much closer to home such as masturbation or sodomy. The eighteenth-century synonym for onanism or masturbation was 'self-pollution', a term which captures the inherently auto-destructive quality associated with this 'solitary vice', one widely believed to lead to enfeeblement, insanity, and even death if it was not ruthlessly stamped out.

Mosse argues that the manly ideal shows remarkable resilience throughout the modern era and suggests that it does not begin to break down until the 1950s. In its idealized form, masculinity undergoes many local revisions and permutations but nevertheless many of the same features seem to occur again and again, as if the image were a necessary fiction in constant need of refurbishment or updating. This comes through in Jünger's reflections on the terrible aftermath of the battle of the Somme in *The Storm of Steel* where, side by side with a picture of the devastation of the landscape – a 'fantastic desert' of shell-holes 'strewn with bully-tins, broken weapons, fragments of uniform, and dud shells, with one or two dead bodies on its edge' – we witness the emergence of a new man, 'more mysterious and hardy and callous than in any previous battle'. For Jünger this figure signalled the death of chivalry and the old Europe:

> After this battle the German soldier wore the steel helmet, and in his features there were chiselled the lines of an energy stretched to the utmost pitch, lines that future generations will

perhaps find as fascinating and imposing as those of many
heads of classical or Renaissance times.

(Jünger 1929: 109)

The reference to the classical body is unmistakable. Jünger is
describing a watershed in European experience and yet he still
regards 'honour and gallantry' as crucial if an officer is to be 'the
master of the hour'. In Jünger the manly ideal takes its most heroic
form, an indication perhaps of how difficult it was for modern
masculinity completely to break with the socially redundant codes
of chivalry, as though warriors or knights had not been transformed
into courtiers long ago. 'What is more sublime,' he asks 'than to face
death at the head of a hundred men?' Jünger can imagine nothing
nobler and insists that only weaklings would settle for less. The brave
leader 'will never find obedience fail him, for courage runs through
the ranks like wine' (Jünger 1929: 27).

We will return to the question of heroism in a moment. But
what of those men who did not think like Jünger? How does one
live without the classical body – indeed, couldn't it be said that
the history of modern warfare is precisely what makes that ideal
redundant? For a partial answer we can contrast *The Storm of Steel*
with another book published in the same year, Erich Maria
Remarque's pacificist novel *All Quiet on the Western Front* (1993
[1929]) which provides a view of the German Army from the rank
and file. Although Remarque's book owes more to stories told to
him by other soldiers than to any of his own experiences of the war,
many of the scenes and situations described in *All Quiet on the
Western Front* show an unmistakable resemblance to those recalled
by Jünger: the 'torn, blasted earth' of the battleground littered with
'convulsed and dead soldiers' under a 'greasy sun' (Remarque 1993:
79), for example, or the soldier's sense of the Western Front as 'a
mysterious whirlpool' pulling him 'slowly, irresistibly, inescapably
into itself' (41). For both writers the battle zone seems to have a life
of its own, like some vast lumbering machine or an enormous alien

forcefield against which the individual can easily dwindle into nothing. In each case the narrator recounts his struggle to survive and to find meaning in a world poised at the zero degree of existence.

But in Remarque's novel honour is no longer available to the modern soldier; no glory attaches to his military exploits and, *contra* Mosse, there are few traces of 'the manly qualities of endurance and calmness in battle' (see Mosse 1996: 108). For a brief moment very early on in the book we are given a poignant glimpse of an ancient past in a near magical description of a supply platoon at night in which 'the guns and the wagons' seem to 'float past the dim background of the moonlit landscape' and 'the riders in their steel helmets resemble knights of a forgotten time'. It is a sight that is 'strangely beautiful and arresting', yet the next instant the men are cursing as they stumble around unanticipated shell-holes, falling face-first into the rolls of barbed wire carried by the men in front (43).

Where Jünger sought to cultivate an almost spiritual sense of dedication, steeling the body with the unyielding discipline of the mind, Paul, the narrator of *All Quiet on the Western Front*, learns to live inside his body more intensely, shedding the false sentiments inculcated at home and in school. There is a kind of double disillusionment. The harshness of military training quickly quashes any last vestige of idealism – 'we learned that a bright button is weightier than four volumes of Schopenhauer' – and then 'the classical conception of the Fatherland held by our teachers' begins to wither away as the new recruits realize that they are merely being drilled into obedient cannon-fodder. Bursting with enthusiasm, they had enlisted to fight for their country only to discover that they were being prepared 'for heroism as though we were circus-ponies' (20–1).

In fact, the soldiers' experiences turn them into animals of a very different stamp. They become 'wild beasts', 'because that is the only thing which brings us through safely': in battle, if one wants 'to live at any price', this 'is a sheer necessity' (78, 94). The need to survive teaches these men 'the indifference of wild creatures', transforming them 'into unthinking animals in order to give [them] the weapon of instinct', for had they relied upon 'clear, conscious thought' the shock of fully understanding the grim reality of war would have driven them to the point of mental breakdown (178). This state of bestiality moves through several distinct registers. In one characterization, it involves stripping away the folly and irrelevance of modern culture in order to recognize the animal nature that is the true essence of humankind. On other occasions, such as close proximity to battle, man's animality is conceived as a wilful slide into 'degeneration', voluntarily embracing the condition of so-called primitive peoples like the 'Bushmen', abandoning the entire process of social development that is supposed to separate tribal societies from twentieth-century Europeans (179). Or again, soldiering on may be depicted as a brutalized deepening of the unconscious, a retreat from the rational mind by forcing the 'terror of the front' to 'sink down in us like a stone' through an elaborate effort of repression (94–5). The same stark bestial reality afflicts the enemy too and one of the most striking features of Remarque's book is how little national differences really matter. Even in defeat, animal imagery comes to the fore: Russian prisoners-of-war, 'big fellows with beards' seem to resemble 'meek, scolded, St. Bernard dogs' (125)

Underlying each of these ideas of the 'human animal' is a view of the male body as 'grotesque': uncontrolled, appetitive, vulgar, dirty and inconvenient, a body that smells and bleeds and laughs and screams, especially when it is not supposed to. It stands, of course, in stark contrast to the virtues of the classical body, beautifully proportioned, nobly disposed, and perfectly ordered, whether represented by Winckelmann's Greek revivalism or Jünger's military discipline. In *All Quiet on the Western Front*, however, bodily functions are ever-present: soldiers wet their beds, curse and grind their teeth, and their bodies gurgle horribly as the life oozes slowly from them. We learn of the pleasures of sitting on the portable latrines in the middle of a field of poppies, reading, smoking and playing cards. And that a 'sharpened spade' makes a better weapon than a bayonet, because it can easily be removed from the opponent's body without having 'to kick hard on the other fellow's belly to pull it out again' (72).

The grotesque body foregrounds 'the gaping mouth, the protuberant belly and buttocks, the feet and the genitals' (Stallybrass and White 1986: 22). 'The soldier is on friendlier terms than other men with his stomach and intestines', observes Paul, and he also notices that 'three-quarters of [a soldier's] vocabulary is derived from these regions', giving 'an intimate flavour to expressions of his greatest joy as well as of his deepest indignation' (Remarque 1993: 11). Everything in war has a visceral, earthy quality about it and the messiness of daily life can be a source of pleasure as well as anxiety. From Remarque's depiction of the Western Front it is clear that Napoleon was only half-right when he said that an army marches on its stomach: here it thinks with its belly too.

The opposition between the classical and the grotesque body was initially theorized by the Russian literary critic Mikhail Bakhtin (1895–1975) in his magisterial study *Rabelais and His World* (1965) which reads the Renaissance writer's huge sprawling text *Gargantua and Pantagruel* as an attempt to dismantle the stifling orthodoxies inherited from the Middle Ages. According to Bakhtin, Rabelais' assault on the high seriousness of medieval scholasticism uses a bawdy and exaggerated treatment of the human body as an occasion for humour and parody. 'Laughter degrades and materializes', says Bakhtin; it deflates the empty pretensions of the spiritual and the transcendental and brings them down to earth (Bakhtin 1968: 20). Rabelais' style can be termed 'grotesque realism' or 'grotesque fantasy' since it describes excessive and outrageous events with an extraordinary visual exactness. This is as true of the tumultuous battle scenes in the book as it is of the story of Gargantua's birth following his mother's attack of diarrhoea after eating too much tripe.

While Remarque's novel is a far cry from this kind of overripe comedy, it does take the indignities and satisfactions experienced by the male body as the butt of much bitter humour and even aggression. The grotesque masculinity of Paul and his comrades is partly defined by their irreverance, which often erupts into insubordination. Officers who are perceived as vindictive or unjust are likely to be subjected to humiliating reprisals, as in the case of Corporal Himmelstoss, 'the strictest disciplinarian in the camp' (Remarque 1993: 21). Ambushed on his way back from the pub, Himmelstoss is tied up and horsewhipped until his 'striped . . . backside gleamed in the moonlight' as he scampers off 'on all fours' (38). What makes *All Quiet on the Western Front* a pacifist text is not any outright condemnation of violence *per se*, for the stories of revenge or retaliation that it tells positively revel in cruelty and pain. Instead, it is as if the men's aggression must first be redirected against the enemy within their own ranks in order that the book's critique of the institution of war can be underwritten by an appeal to a common humanity. The realization that 'you [the enemy] are a man like me' depends upon a prior displacement of hostility, upon *someone*, *somewhere* bearing the burden of difference and hatred, upon guilt and blame being re-assigned in order to secure the creation of innocence (147).

There are two obvious problems with linking masculinity and the grotesque body in this way, however well it might seem to fit the account of army life in Remarque's novel. First, why should we assume that the grotesque body is some special preserve of men? Indeed, doesn't the example of Gargantua's unfortunate mother with her prolapsed bowel suggest that women are equally likely to be depicted in similar terms, just as the statue of Venus de Milo represents the classical womanly body? This is a perfectly fair point – and for an exploration of this important topic, see Mary Russo's excellent study *The Female Grotesque* (1995) – but it is one that neither Bakhtin nor his disciples would wish to deny. Instead, they could plausibly argue that the classical and the grotesque body each has its own distinctively masculine *and* feminine variants. For every Corporal Himmelstoss in a book like *All Quiet on the Western Front*, there is a Bertha Mason in *Jane Eyre*.

However, this response leads on to the second query. Because, put like this, it sounds as if the classical and the grotesque are timeless categories – as though, for example, the image of the coarse, farting, scratching, yawning, boozing male persists unchanged from Rabelais' Gargantua to more recent incarnations like Gary and Tony in the TV series *Men Behaving Badly*. Doesn't this merely show that Paul and his fellow-soldiers in *All Quiet on the Western Front* were correct in claiming that ultimately human beings (and men especially) are merely animals? To this objection the answer has to be: yes and no. It is undoubtedly true that there are continuities in low or rough humour over the ages and that the infirmities of the body will always be a subject of laughter and derision. But on the other hand, what is thought of as vulgar or in bad taste will very much depend upon the standards of polite society in different times and places. And, to return to the two examples that we have been discussing, there is a world of difference between Rabelais and Remarque. As we noted in passing, Rabelais' writing involves more than making lewd jokes at the expense of the other-worldly monk or the medieval philosopher, for hand in hand with the farcical distortions of human bodily functions we find an exceptionally precise anatomical knowledge of its workings.

The point about 'Rabelaisian laughter', argues Bakhtin, is not only that it 'destroys traditional connections and abolishes idealized strata; it also brings out the crude, unmediated connections between things that people otherwise seek to keep separate, in pharasaical error' (Bakhtin 1981 [1975]: 170). The idea of the infant Gargantua finding his own way out of his mother's womb by climbing up a hollow vein and easing himself out through her left ear is a patently ridiculous conceit, but it is rendered in scrupulous physiological detail. Set beside this meticulous order of description, Remarque's style seems loose and impressionistic. Rabelais' fascination with the life of the body is part of a humanist outlook that conferred the highest value upon ordinary human existence. Paradoxically, this often results in comic representations of death, of the 'cheerfully dying man', 'presented in close relationship with the birth of new life and – simultaneously – with laughter', not to mention food, drink and 'sexual indecencies'. Despite its many bloody and chaotic episodes, *Gargantua and Pantagruel* is largely motivated by the desire to valorize 'the eternal triumph' of life over death, to insist on the human 'responsibility to fight to the end for this life' (Bakhtin 1981: 197–8).

One would be hard pressed to find an instance of 'cheerful death' in *All Quiet on the Western Front*. Although the role of vulgarity in Remarque's novel is to undermine the pieties of Germany's official culture, it provides little basis for optimism. The war has so disrupted the experience of the book's protagonists that they are torn between the struggle to stay alive and their sense that death will bring a welcome relief from their suffering. Some of the bleakest moments in the novel record their feeling of being isolated from the sympathetic understanding of other men, cut adrift from past and future generations, from those who never knew and those who will all too quickly forget: these 'weary, broken, burnt out, rootless' soldiers will finally be 'superfluous even to ourselves' (Remarque 1993: 190). In Remarque the grotesque male body is part of a language of refusal, of resistance to the sanitized ideologies of the state; but, as the novel wears on, the body increasingly takes on another kind of grotesqueness due to its having been disfigured or dismembered. Even in hospital 'the wounded have their shattered limbs hanging free in the air from a gallows' or their 'intestine wounds . . . are constantly full of excreta' (172). To find a visual equivalent of these scenes, one would need to turn to the shattered bodies and twisted faces displayed in Otto Dix's paintings of the Great War and its aftermath, particularly his gruesomely stylized portraits of crippled war veterans (see Armstrong 1998: 96–7).

DISSIPATION AND 'NATURAL CHARACTER'

So far we have been tracing the history of 'the manly ideal' and its countertypes in the modern era, looking especially closely at changing conceptions of the male body as it was re-imagined following the First World War. One disadvantage of Mosse's account of the dominant form of masculinity – and this is also true of the opposition between the classical and the grotesque – is that, however closely these contrasting figures are intertwined, they can easily start to become polarized, as if they were mutually exclusive. In fact, masculinities are often much more inherently contradictory than such an analysis would tend to suggest, and never more so than in periods of intense social upheaval. 'I'll nearly always be mistaken if I think that a man has only a single character', wrote the young Stendhal in his diary in 1801 (Beyle 1955: 14). Mosse may well be right about the manly ideal, but wrong to think of it in such a relatively rigid manner. By regarding it as 'a stereotype, presenting a standardized mental picture', Mosse sometimes comes close to reifying his own argument unnecessarily (Mosse 1996: 5).

As we saw earlier, Mosse dates the origins of the new manly ideal from the second half of the eighteenth century and this period therefore provides an interesting test case as to how robust this male sense of self was in practice. London in the eighteenth century was a highly contested social space in which a number of social groupings and factions vied for power and in the city's theatres, taverns, and coffee-houses several different styles of masculinity were to be seen, among them the fop, the rake and the gentleman, to name just a handful. None of these labels was entirely clear-cut and few kept the same meaning for very long; as chronicled in early issues of periodicals like *The Tatler*, for example, they were 'less an orderly taxonomy than a fluid continuum of male gender types' usually distinguished through 'details in the extravagance of their dress' and by the ways in which they sought the favours of women (McKeon 1995: 313).

To make one's way in such a volatile milieu was not always easy. One of the best case studies we have of the uncertainties surrounding masculinity in the middle of the century comes from the diaries kept by James Boswell, whose *Life of Johnson* (1791) was one of the first modern biographies. Throughout his diaries Boswell worried over his ambitions and his failings, and about what kind of man he really wanted to be. His *London Journal 1762–1763* is particularly fascinating because of his descriptions of the wealth of opportunities and temptations that the capital made available to him: it was, as he disarmingly observes, simultaneously 'the seat of Parliament and the seat of pleasure' (Boswell 1950: 140). Boswell, who sometimes dreamed of a career in government, found himself attracted to both, yet he also believed that they were quite incompatible. Unfortunately, he found it hard to decide which mattered most.

Boswell's dilemma can be read as at once social and philosophical. Socially, Boswell came from a wealthy, landed family of considerable professional standing: his father was one of five judges in Scotland's supreme criminal court and as a young man Boswell was pressed into studying law, which he did with little enthusiasm. By the late 1750s he had already begun to publish his own verse and, much to his father's dismay, he formed the plan of becoming an officer in the Guards – not because he had any desire to fight for his country, but simply to enable him to live permanently in London. In fact, following the successful conclusion of the Seven Years' War, the army already had far more officers than it needed and Boswell's aspirations were hopelessly unrealistic. But his experiences in the city, where he met the writer Samuel Johnson for the first time, played a key role in his formation as a man of letters.

On an ethical or philosophical level, Boswell was tormented by questions of identity that ultimately derived from strains in the way the self could be imagined in the late eighteenth century. Boswell aspired to be a man who 'was rational and composed, yet lively and entertaining'. But in spite of a firm belief that his 'natural character is that of dignity', he found it difficult to 'fix myself in such a character and preserve it uniformly' and when his 'resolution' or will-power faltered he became a 'dissipated, inconstant fellow' at the mercy of every passing whim or fancy (Boswell 1950: 258). Boswell alternates between seeing himself as a sober, upright individual, a condition he describes as *retenu* – that is to say, reserved or restrained – and feeling that his best self is always being thwarted by his own uncontrollable enthusiasms or impulses, rendering him scatter-brained or *étourdi*, a man whose identity lacked a secure centre, a slave to his emotions.

Could the self ever be anything more than a loose bundle of appetites or sensations, without a stable core? Some of Boswell's contemporaries, like his friend the philosopher David Hume, were sceptical that it could. But, while Boswell resisted this idea intellectually – hence his conviction that each man possessed a 'natural character', a kind of essential inner self – he found himself pulled between the competing models of masculinity he encountered in London. In this period, Boswell:

> represents an amalgam of increasingly mobile status positions: he vacillates between Scots, English, aristocratic, and bourgeois male identities as he maintains his dignity, attempts to adhere to a strict sexual morality, and pursues the pleasure that may constitute the privilege of his station.
>
> (Weed 1997/8: 216)

He is, by turns, pious and amorous, a man of gravitas and a man of sensual pleasures, a highminded scholar who will sometimes masquerade as a lower-class tradesman. Paradoxically, the sexual desires that are partly aroused by the urge to transgress class boundaries are then immediately punished by his own self-disgust at having done so. On one occasion he 'picked up a strong, jolly young damsel' and, after walking her down to Westminster Bridge, found that '[t]he whim of doing it there with the Thames rolling below us amused me much. Yet after the brutish appetite was sated,

I could not but despise myself for being so closely united with such a low wretch' (Boswell 1950: 255–6).

As Felicity Nussbaum's detailed study has shown, the contrast between Boswell's *retenu* and *étourdi* selves was deeply gendered. His rationality and his reserve are not just confirmed by the approval of his male peers; they also crucially depend upon his 'power to maintain dominance over women' (Nussbaum 1989: 115). In the account of his affair with the actress he calls Louisa in his journal, Boswell writes of his 'sweet delirium' and 'supreme rapture'. Yet, although he is thoroughly delighted by his own 'godlike vigour', his self-possession prevents him from losing control, from frittering away his precious masculinity. His phrasing here is particularly revealing. 'Sobriety', he insists, 'preserved me from effeminacy and weakness' (Boswell 1950: 139). A week later, however, on discovering the painful signs of an unwanted foreign visitor, 'Signor Gonorrhea', he has second thoughts and is beside himself at the idea of having been 'the dupe of a strumpet', at having wasted his time and his money (155–6).

Believing that Louisa must have known of the infection, Boswell confronts her. Once again he is in command of the situation: 'I really behaved with a manly composure and polite dignity that could not fail to inspire an awe', while Louisa stands miserably before him as 'pale as ashes and trembled and faltered'. He receives her denials and anxious queries about his health in silence, dismissing her from his mind as 'a most consummate dissembling whore'. Boswell refuses to accept any blame for this incident, regarding his misfortune as 'merely the chance of war'. And so the affair is over. But what happens next sheds fresh light on the relationship between Boswell's rival selves.

On leaving Louisa, he calls on someone much older than himself, the actor David Garrick. Boswell was to seek the approval of fatherly men all his life and is terribly flattered when this rich and famous figure confidently predicts that one day his visitor will be 'very great'. Yet Boswell is too anxious and disconsolate to allow himself to imagine such a future. Instead, he becomes 'what the French call *un étourdi*' and gives 'free vent' to his feelings of admiration for Garrick, seizing him by the hand and heaping affection and gratitude upon the actor. This emotional outburst raises 'a charming flutter of spirits' and relieves his depression. Nevertheless, on returning to his lodgings at the end of the day, he again feels 'very bad' (160–2).

In the eyes of the modern reader Boswell might appear as a muddled, rather vain individual, prone to overpowering mood-swings. However, what distinguishes Boswell's psychological universe from our own is the way in which he has to tack between contrasting styles of masculinity in order to neutralize his feelings of guilt and shame and continue to believe in his own self-worth. Boswell's emotional economy is a tangle of nuances and discriminations, a delicate balancing act that can easily fall apart. To be 'un étourdi' can be compromising, but it is not necessarily to be despised, so long as a sense of proportion is maintained. There is a world of difference between the warm eloquent (not to say, homosocial) candour that passes between men, whether among one's peers or one's betters, and finding oneself unmanned in the presence of a woman. In one desperate episode, Boswell deliberately kits himself out in the scruffy attire of 'a blackguard', pretending to be 'a disbanded officer of the Royal Volunteers', though he also describes himself to the prostitutes he is seeking as 'a barber' and 'a highwayman'. After a dispiriting tale of rejection turning to rape, Boswell is pleased to report that his clothes and his lies never prevented him from being recognized as 'a gentleman in disguise' by those on whom he bestows his favours (272–3). If self-loathing is never very far away, some of his most dissolute nocturnal adventures can still occasionally confirm him in his preferred identity.

In Boswell's journals, despite the desire for an essential or 'natural character', we see the author repeatedly returning to the idea that the self is not fixed, but 'may be continually revised and remade' (Nussbaum 1989: 107). In his *Life of Johnson* Boswell produced an account of an exemplary life, 'a man whose talents, acquirements, and virtues, were so extraordinary, that the more his character is considered, the more he will be regarded by the present age, and by posterity, with admiration and reverence' (Boswell 1953: 1402). Above all others, Dr Johnson was the companion whose advice most consistently helped to raise Boswell's spirits and to give him a sense of purpose, for Johnson's pre-eminence as a writer and scholar had only been achieved after many setbacks. In return, Boswell's biography aimed to establish Johnson as a literary icon, an inspiration for future generations.

'THE HERO AS MAN OF LETTERS'

This was not to be. By the mid-nineteenth century, Johnson's character had already been turned into caricature and he was remembered as a man whose fabulous eccentricities seemed to mark him out as a figure of fun, one whose 'opinions' were 'fast becoming obsolete' (Carlyle 1966 [1841]: 182). It was left to another Scottish writer, Thomas Carlyle, to attempt to rescue Johnson's reputation and he did so by presenting an image that stood in sharp contrast to Boswell's and that was part of a new take on the 'manly ideal' tailored to the altered circumstances of the Victorian age. Less than eighty years after Boswell and Johnson had first met in the capital, Carlyle chose to deliver his annual course of lectures in London on the topic of 'heroes', those 'Great Men' who had shaped the course of 'Universal History'. And among the curiously assorted names in his pantheon – Mohammed, Luther, Cromwell, Rousseau – Carlyle numbered the undervalued Johnson as a hero of a new type, 'the hero as man of letters'.

Carlyle's survey identified six categories of hero, some of whom, like mythical or divine beings, prophets and priests, were largely bound to the past, while others, such as the poets Dante and Shakespeare, lived on in the present by continuing to give a national voice to their peoples. But with the coming of print culture a new kind of hero becomes possible, raising some of the functions of the idols of yesteryear to a higher level. The printing press enables the man of letters to reach out across time and space and 'accomplish *miracles*': 'teaching, preaching, governing, and all else' (160–1). For in Carlyle's view it is the writer whose books and essays now instruct the nation and who is therefore best able to make things happen, displacing the pulpit, the university and parliament from power. In an intoxicating flight of rhetoric, Carlyle imagines the man of letters as representating a new ruling class, one that would place 'intellect at the top of affairs' and ensure government by 'the true, just, humane and valiant man' (169).

Carlyle paints the lives of his heroes in intensely dramatic colours. They are typically men of humble origins, earnestly wrestling with immense obstacles in an endeavour to find and realize the truth. They are sincere, honest, determined, fearless, and free of all humbug or cant. Often these qualities are instinctive: Shakespeare, remembered here as a writer of tragedies and 'a blessed heaven-sent Bringer of Light', was 'everyway an unconscious man', 'a Force of Nature'. For, intones Carlyle in his best biblical manner, 'whatsoever is truly great' in a man 'springs-up from the *in*articulate deeps' (111–12). As this lofty standpoint implies, Carlyle's sketch of Johnson is a far cry from the 'highly instructive and highly entertaining' conversationalist described by Boswell (Boswell 1950: 292). Instead it depicts him as a tragic individual struggling heroically against every kind of adversity, his noble inner nature beset by poverty, ill-health and neglect:

> Figure him there, with his scrofulous diseases, with his great greedy heart, and unspeakable chaos of thoughts; stalking mournful as a stranger in this Earth; eagerly devouring what spiritual thing he could come at: school-languages and other merely grammatical stuff, if there were nothing better! The largest soul that was in all England; and provision made for it of 'fourpence-halfpenny a day.' Yet a giant invincible soul; a true man's.
>
> (Carlyle 1966: 179)

Johnson is hardly Cromwell or Mohammed; but Carlyle gives his work an epic grandeur that blurs the differences between them, transforming him into a crusader against scepticism and unbelief. And, as the lectures draw to a close, one is finally unsure in whose hands Carlyle expects the future to lie: the man of letters or the man of action.

With hindsight it is hard not to read Carlyle's attempt to depict the writer's vocation in heroic vein as a vindication of his own personal myth of authorship, a reworking of the narrative of his struggle to carve out a literary career for himself. 'To carve out' is no idle figure of speech here, for one crucial move in Carlyle's creation of a distinctive literary persona was his alignment of the writer's work with the simple dignity of his father's daily labour as a stone-mason. Carlyle's memoir of his father's life, written immediately after news of his death in 1832, uses the same language of heroic struggle as the 1840 lectures: 'Nothing that he undertook to do but he did it faithfully and like a true man' (Carlyle 1881: 5). Revealingly, Carlyle even compares him to the man of letters, surmising that his father was 'among Scottish peasants what Samuel Johnson was among English authors' (15).

As Norma Clarke has argued, one effect of this Oedipal identification was to reclaim the world of literature for men, to produce a 'social fiction' to offset the social fact of increased opportunities and recognition for women writers in the early decades of the nineteenth century (Clarke 1991: 41). In Carlyle's imagination such brave, reverent, natural men formed a kind of brotherhood, united in devotion to their calling. This trope of brotherhood appears in a variety of guises in Victorian art and literature, from the pre-Raphaelites to Bram Stoker's *Dracula*. At times this kinship between men is compared to a monastic order, as in Carlyle's meditation in *Past and Present* (1843) on the contrast between the 'wretchedness' of the modern workhouse and the life that was once found in the now ruined abbey at Bury St Edmunds (Carlyle 1971: 262). In this text, as elsewhere in Carlyle's writings, women are pushed to the margins of the ideal society, at which point they can be conveniently forgotten. In *Past and Present* the symbolic moment for this exclusion occurs when the young Samson, the man who will become the monastery's abbot and heroic leader, leaves his mother for the Church.

Carlyle's fantasy of male-bonding is not without its problems, however. The powerful communal feelings passing between men can become charged with desire and, at St Edmundsbury, it is the task of the fatherly abbot to set an example, to hold their psychic energies in check, and to sublimate any last trace of homoeroticism into productive work. The nobility of the Carlylean male ideal is compromised by a deep interior division between the need for mastery or control that will create order out of chaos and a fear of the potentially untameable flows of energy within. One can see this as a splitting of gendered identity, in which the instability of what for the early Victorians constituted 'maleness', the potent physical powers that were thought to be of the basic essence of man, begins to sabotage the 'manliness' or self-discipline with which an individual conducts himself. For Carlyle,

> maleness, potentially progressive, is also innately diseased. The very spring of male identity is also potentially the source of its destruction as dissolution. Repelled by the male body, by male sexuality, by what he sees as the miasmic swamp of the male psyche, Carlyle imagines the interior of the male as polluted, unclean. Masculine energy may power the energy of industrial society but it may also disrupt it in a power surge, an overflow of the diseased fluid interior in a flood that would dissolve the ego boundaries of the male self and the patriarchal bounds of the social system.
>
> (Sussman 1995: 24)

Herbert Sussman's analysis of the phantasmatic construction of masculinity in texts like *Past and Present* brings out not only Carlyle's immensely fertile strategy of yoking together materials drawn from different historical times, so that the warrior may be reborn (or re-branded) as the 'Captain of Industry'; but it also reveals the extreme precariousness of his restless imaginings, a masculine ideal that is in constant danger of collapsing under the weight of its own contradictions. Unlike the rival images of the male self held out for inspection in Boswell's journals, this is not so much a conflict between competing masculinities as a strong bid to establish a dominant form of masculinity for the industrial era that pays the price of its own exclusions. Carlyle's dreams contain the seeds of his own worst nightmares, haunted by thoughts of indolence or disruption that assume the shapes of feminized men (the lazy freed slave conjured up in the notorious pamphlet 'The Nigger Question') or castrating women (the female marauders depicted in his study *The French Revolution*).

We would seem to have moved a long way from the battlefields and the trenches. But in fact we have come full circle. For one of the major influences upon Sussman's account of Carlyle in his book *Victorian Masculinities* is Klaus Theweleit's disturbing two-volume study *Male Fantasies* (1987, 1989), an investigation into the gendered imaginary of the right wing *Freikorps*, private armies of mercenaries that were employed to contain the 'threat' of communism in the aftermath of the First World War. From an intensive reading of letters, autobiographies and novels, Theweleit reconstructs the fantasy world of these forerunners of German fascism showing how it thrived upon a series of pathological representations of hostile and aggressive women who symbolized all that was felt to be most terrifying in their political adversaries. Here sexual predators and militant revolutionaries became indistinguishable: the mocking, brazen prostitute was sister to the sadistic communist rifle-woman, phallic creatures who brought slow, sexually humiliating death, finally leaving their male victims 'drenched in black blood between hips and thighs' (Theweleit 1987: 74).

Blood flows throughout these texts. But so too do desire, energy, tears, and bile, passions and bodily fluids. Bodies themselves seem to merge into a liquid mass, the 'Red flood' that threatens to drown the gallant men who are defending their nation's honour. Theweleit traces a complicated psychic economy of dams and torrents in which the battle to stem the swelling enemy tide has as its counterpart the soldier's strict control over his own bodily functions so that he does not turn to water, jelly or shit. Unlike the sublimated, productive energy that courses through Carlyle's imagery, the literature of the *Freikorps* typically erupts into climactic violence when the moment is right. In one scene depicted by the popular novelist Edwin Erich Dwinger, the men cannot shoot:

> into the crowd of women until the advance wave of that slimy stream is already upon them. Not until the spit of one of the working-class women is already dripping down his medal of honour does Donat [the soldier] fire into the woman's open mouth. And not until then does Donat perceive that what was once a face is now only a bloody pulp.
>
> (quoted in Theweleit 1987: 428–9)

In this hideous contra-flow, aggression is always already sexualized and the metonymic slippage between different kinds of fluids – slime, spit, blood, pulp – is endless. In Theweleit's analysis, the appeal of fascism goes right to the heart of this desperately embattled masculine imagination, for the Nazis, in effect, promised to turn the tide, channel men's energies and desires, 'and let them flow inside their rituals' (429). Fascism thus 'translates internal states into massive external monuments or ornaments' (431); it offers a controlled release of intolerable frustrations through mass political spectacles like the Nuremberg Rally.

As a theory of fascism, Theweleit's argument is tendentious in the extreme. It would reduce too many complex political and economic events, from hyperinflation to the anti-Jewish pogroms of the Reichskristallnacht, to an immense psychodrama. But as a study of what we might call a *combatant masculinity*, one that acquired a deadly social presence at a key point in German history, Theweleit's work is extremely insightful, not least for the way in which it seeks to identify the ideological currents that passed back and forth between personal memories, popular literature, and political propaganda. It allows us to glimpse the inner dynamic through which the classic military body patriotically extolled by Ernst Jünger came to be transformed into the fascist 'new man'.

Jünger, Remarque, Boswell and Carlyle were all engaged in an attempt to imagine a form of manhood that was worthy of the name, to construct a version of the male self that could command moral and cultural respect, sometimes in the face of the most appalling conditions. Yet despite the fact that their work can be placed within a general history of the dominant modes of masculinity in Western Europe, these writers differ considerably in their accounts of men's strengths and blindspots. Taken together, their writings show more signs of discontinuity than convergence. They cast doubt on the notion of a single modern manly ideal.

Even where there are points of overlap, as in the profound ambivalence towards bourgeois society that they each exhibit, the differences between them outweigh the similarities. One of the most unsettling episodes in *All Quiet on the Western Front* comes when the soldiers are sent on leave and are unable to adjust to civilian life. Not only do they find themselves estranged from the people who remained in their home towns, but ordinary everyday sounds like the noise of the tramcars remind them of the screech of shells whistling across the battlefield. The mood of despair evoked by Remarque is diametrically opposed to the scathing tone adopted by Jünger in his indictment of 'the bourgeois epoch' a mere two years later. In a highly polemical essay 'On Danger' (1931) Jünger attacked the bourgeois as the person who overvalues security, who desires a reasonable world from which risk, misfortune and chance have been completely banished. The comfortable middle classes are not only unaware that life is becoming increasingly hazardous, but they are ill-equipped to understand why this is to be welcomed. In their eyes the man who jubilantly volunteered to fight for his country in the Great War was guilty of 'patriotic error or a suspect love of adventure'; whereas, in reality, 'this jubilation was a revolutionary protest against the values of the bourgeois world', a Nietzschean demand for 'a revaluation of all values'. Jünger places the warrior alongside the other great outsiders of modernity, the artist and the criminal, men who, whether 'lofty or base', are closer to 'the elemental' nature of things than their bourgeois cousins (Jünger 1993 [1931]).

OF BEETLES AND DANDIES

Jünger believed 'the values of the bourgeois world' to be incompatible with what he called 'the select embodiments of a powerful masculinity' and on one occasion he even went so far as to depict combat as 'the male form of procreation' (quoted in Huyssen 1993: 10). But by no means every writer who has found himself at odds with modern bourgeois society has regarded it as lacking in masculinity. To the contrary, for some modernist writers it is the crushingly oppressive nature of bourgeois masculinity that led to its symbolic renunciation in the pages of their fiction.

As an extreme example, consider one of the most famous of all twentieth-century texts: Franz Kafka's novella *The Metamorphosis* (1915) with its abrupt and unforgettable opening: 'When Gregor Samsa awoke one morning from troubled dreams he found himself transformed in his bed into a monstrous insect' (Kafka 1992: 76). At first sight Kafka's fable would seem to have little to do with gender, and Gregor Samsa's downward spiral from rejection by his family to an ignominious death has often been read as a parable of spiritual alienation and martyrdom, a vivid allegory of the human condition. However, recent Kafka scholarship has begun to think much harder about the author's relationship to the time and place within which he worked, producing a very different picture of these strange, disquieting writings.

In his fascinating book *Kafka's Clothes* (1992), Mark M. Anderson portrays the young Kafka as a contradictory figure, a dandyish man about town who was nevertheless deeply critical of the decadence of urban life. Although early photographs show him 'sporting broad, upturned collars, fancy silk neckties, even a top hat, tuxedo, and gloves', he was also attending popular lectures on clothing reform and the need for a wholesale return to nature (51). Both of these preoccupations had an impact upon Kafka's aestheticism for, while he soon ceased to cultivate the stylish air of the snappy dresser, his single-minded pursuit of a life *in* art led him ruthlessly to strip away each and every diversion or encumbrance, including the possibility of a happy marriage, until he had reached the point where he could describe himself as 'made of literature' and 'nothing else' (quoted 95). And, of course, Kafka's purism, like the dandyism which it replaced, was a far cry from the bustling commercial ethos of his father's affluent fancy-goods store. It provided a way of distinguishing himself from the Jewish milieu into which he was born, distancing him from the world of his parents.

With this cultural context in mind, Anderson reads *The Metamorphosis* as the difficult incarnation of what he calls 'a will toward art' (131), the desire to move into a 'self-enclosed world of aesthetic play and freedom' represented by the symmetries of Gregor's insect form (142). (Notwithstanding his differences from Kafka, it is perhaps worth recalling here that, besides literature and war, one of Ernst Jünger's other great passions was to scour the world in search of rare beetles, discovering species whose teeming variety seemed to offer endless scope for aesthetic contemplation.) Previous interpretations of Kafka's novella have tended to focus upon the anxieties accompanying Gregor's transformation and have often failed to take into account the pleasures that his new body evidently brings him. As soon as he is able to place his legs firmly on the ground, for example, Gregor at once begins to experience 'a sense of physical well-being', an instinctive 'joy' in the discovery of an unexpected capacity for movement; and later he learns to enjoy 'hanging from the ceiling', gently swaying to and fro, a delightful manoeuvre that allows him to 'breathe more freely' (Kafka 1992: 89,

101). In such brief, bitter-sweet moments he seems finally to have transcended the care-worn routines of the ordinary commercial traveller he once was.

As the story makes clear, in his human phase Gregor had been chained to his family and his job, forced to become the household's breadwinner after the failure of his father's business. Both institutions are intensely exploitative. No sooner has the company discovered that Gregor has missed the early morning train than the chief clerk is knocking on the door of the family's apartment to find out where their employee has got to. But, most sinister of all, Gregor's father starts to undergo his own monstrous transformation, changing from a semi-invalid apparently defeated by life into a large, vigorous, uniformed patriarch who drives him away with his stick, bombarding Gregor with apples and hastening his death. Indeed, for Anderson, the father's new uniform, together with other textual details such as the three anonymous bearded men who later become the Samsa family's lodgers, are signs of a highly regimented form of social existence from which Gregor is permitted to escape. One could argue that Gregor must ultimately die because there is literally no place for him in this soulless, grasping world.

Several commentators have drawn attention to the ways in which the metamorphosed Gregor has also been effectively feminized. He has lost his social position as the real head of the household and consequently is banished from public view. His voice immediately begins to change – Eric Santner describes Gregor's 'distressed chirping' as 'the mutation of the male voice in the direction of the feminine' – and as the story develops he becomes increasingly vulnerable and passive (Santner 1996: 206). There even seems to be a curious parallel between Gregor's newly 'curved brown belly' and the image of the 'harem women' with which he identifies the other commercial travellers who are far lazier in their habits than he is (Kafka 1992: 76–7). However, it might be more accurate to say, not that Gregor is in the process of taking on female attributes, but rather that he has become unable to continue to live up to the demands of masculinity that have been his lot in life until now. In *The Metamorphosis* there is a kind of withdrawal from, or divestment of, a conventionally dutiful bourgeois masculinity – a disengagement that is later given a surprising justification when we learn that the Samsa family is not really bankrupt at all. If one implication of *The Metamorphosis* is that the true artist cannot flourish in such a brazenly commercial world, another no less sobering reflection is surely that the modern codes of masculinity are based upon an illusion. In the Oedipal dramas played out in Kafka's fictional universe, relations between fathers and sons are always unstable and liable to take unexpected turns for the worse. Once Gregor is gone family morale among the Samsas revives and the story closes with happy thoughts of Gregor's sister finding 'a good husband' (126), a new 'son' who will erase all memory of Gregor's unmanly failings.

Ranging from the aggressiveness of writers like Jünger and Carlyle to the retreat from gendered identity in *The Metamorphosis*, the snapshots assembled in this chapter suggest something of the historical variability in the forms that masculinity has assumed when it has been imagined and explored through different kinds of literary texts. Fashioning masculinities *in writing* appears as a complex and precarious enterprise, in which any claim to fix upon a core of manly attributes has always had to be placed and justified within a wider field of cultural differences. Indeed, the uncertainties and self-doubts attending Boswell's struggle to discover exactly what sort of man he most wanted to be indicate just how fluid the regulative ideals of masculinity, not to mention the fantasies underpinning them, could sometimes be. To do full justice to this order of complexity we need, as Christopher Lane has eloquently put it, 'a less defined and infinitely messier sense of process, of ideas being worked out in texts trying to make clear their own understanding of desire, intimacy, and gender' (Lane 1999: xxi). Terms like 'masculinity' and 'femininity' carry an immense amount of cultural baggage, but they can also cover up far more than they reveal. Though conventionally regarded as a set of mutually exclusive binary opposites that constitute the bedrock of experience, it is possible that these categories are too restricted, too simplistic, too crude even to serve as an adequate shorthand for the pleasures of the body, let alone to be taken for granted as cultural or human universals. The next chapter considers some of the recent debates that take this possibility seriously.

3

QUEERING THE PITCH

Kafka's Gregor Samsa represents one version of masculinity's vanishing-point. Here is another: after the British Football Association had charged two rival players with misconduct following a fight during a match between Chelsea and Liverpool in February 1999, the man who threw the first punch alleged that he had been provoked by his opponent's cries of: 'Come on, come on, give it to me up the arse.' Of course, many would argue that verbal abuse is simply an inevitable part of a highly competitive game which thrives on insults and banter. But there are limits: racist taunts are now officially tolerated much less than they once were, whereas, according to a recent newspaper discussion of this episode, 'homosexuality is still largely seen as a symptom of weakness and thus mercilessly pilloried' (White 1999: 2). The article appeared under the headline 'Queering the pitch', punning on two senses of the word 'queer': as a pejorative term for 'homosexual' and as a verb meaning 'to spoil' or 'to put out of order'.

It is not difficult to see why homosexuality should be the object of what is probably soccer's ultimate taboo. In the name of the game some of the most intense emotional feelings among and between men are openly displayed on the pitch and on the terraces, making football a contact sport in more ways than one. 'I fell in love with football as I was later to fall in love with women', records Nick Hornby at the beginning of *Fever Pitch*, his phenomenally popular evocation of a twenty-year infatuation with the sport; but his earliest memory highlights 'the overwhelming *maleness* of it all' (Hornby 1992: 15–19). To fall in love with 'maleness' as a man falls in love with a woman: Hornby's treatment of football's boredom and its breathtaking highs is far more nuanced than this. Yet it takes only a pinch of exaggeration for an unsympathetic gay critic to discover in the game's mesmeric power 'an essential, deep and graceful masculine mystery of flesh, sweat, skill and leather which non-believers cannot possibly comprehend', a parodic re-description that slyly insinuates a rather different sort of male performance (see Simpson 1996: 34). Football couldn't really be about *that*, could it?

This chapter is about the place of same-sex desire in modern culture, its history and its effects. And foremost among these effects has been the gradual unravelling of any simplistic divide between 'gay' and 'straight', part of a wider recognition that the relation between 'sex' and 'gender' is much more fluid than the division between 'nature' and 'culture' with which these terms are sometimes confused. One of the lessons to be drawn from football's fear that its pitch might be permanently 'queered' by the presence of gay players is an awareness of just how precarious and self-defeating the balancing act required by the game's demand for 'real' men actually is. The dilemma it poses seems inescapable: those who are somehow not masculine enough are obviously suspect and therefore unsuitable. But, on the other hand, men who appear to be *too* masculine are also a problem since there is always the worry that they might have something to hide. We can see traces of this predicament in some of the responses to the public prosecution of Oscar Wilde for what the court called 'acts of gross indecency with another male person', an event which played a decisive role in redefining the acceptable boundaries of gendered identity. Shortly after Wilde's sentence to two years hard labour, the novelist George Gissing – scarcely a gay sympathiser – told a fellow writer:

> I have a theory that he has got into this, not through natural tendency, but simply in deliberate imitation of the old Greek vice. He probably said: go to, let us try the pederastic pleasures, and come to understand them. No doubt whatever he justified himself, both to himself and to others, by classic precedent.
>
> (Gissing 1994 [1895]: 339)

In other words, Gissing thought that Wilde was guilty as charged, but that he had shown lack of judgement rather than evidence of what might have been considered a truly perverted disposition. Oscar Wilde may have been overly influenced by the revival of interest in Hellenic culture – this provided, after all, a language within which such diverse figures as Matthew Arnold and Walter Pater could imagine a renewal of Victorian society – but he was not a 'real' homosexual.

This neo-classical project formed part of Wilde's own self-exculpating rhetoric at the trial when he spoke of 'the love that dare not speak its name . . . that deep spiritual affection that is as pure as it is perfect, and that pervades great works of art, like those of Michelangelo and Shakespeare' (quoted in Cohen 1993: 200).

HOMOSEXUALS, INVERTS AND FAIRIES

Gissing does not use the word 'homosexual' in his letter, perhaps because it was still a relatively new term in 1895; its first appearance in English was probably in an early translation of Krafft-Ebing's sexological compendium *Psychopathia Sexualis* in 1892. By classifying people according to their sexual histories, Krafft-Ebing helped to provide a medical warrant for thinking about sexual acts in terms of pathological types of individuals; or, in Foucault's famous epigram: '[t]he sodomite had been a temporary aberration; the homosexual was now a species' (Foucault 1979: 43). In effect, Gissing's shocked and exasperated defence of Wilde rests on the claim that his behaviour was 'a temporary aberration', that Wilde's un-natural acts were indeed unnatural since they formed no part of his nature.

For much of the twentieth century 'homosexuality' was more than a 'name' that dared not be spoken: within clinical medicine it has been a diagnostic category, a suitable case for treatment, a condition to be cured wherever possible by psychotherapeutic and other, less savoury methods like electro-convulsive therapy. Because of the institutional prestige enjoyed by the medical profession, this way of thinking leached into and strengthened popular beliefs and prejudices about which sexual preferences were acceptable and which were not. It therefore took some time before this terminology could be turned against itself, and 'homosexuality' started 'to demand that its legitimacy or "naturality" be acknowledged', a development aided by liberal sexologists like Havelock Ellis who insisted on viewing 'sexual inversion' as 'a congenital anomaly' rather than as a pathology or sickness (Foucault 1979: 101). As Ellis's analysis suggests, the question of whether homosexuality should be considered as a naturally occurring phenomenon has long been a troubling issue for critics and advocates alike.

How accurate is Foucault's broad contrast between sodomy as a deviant act and the homosexual as a deviant type of individual? It is not hard to find historical examples where same-sex desire seems relatively unproblematic compared to its dominant perception in Western Europe throughout the twentieth century. In the late seventeenth-century 'Song' ('Love a woman? You're an ass') by John Wilmot, the Second Earl of Rochester, the triumphant riposte voiced in the final stanza appears to be free of shame or stigma, despite the poem's evident sense of irony and misogyny:

> Then give me health, wealth, mirth, and wine,
> And if busy Love intrenches,

> There's a sweet, soft page of mine
> Does the trick worth forty wenches.
>
> (Wilmot 1994: 37)

Yet the fact remains that these sentiments derive their impact from their scandalous assault on what would today be (erroneously) understood as heterosexual values ('I'll change a mistress till I'm dead'), values which are more or less taken as given in the bulk of Rochester's poetry. These lines hardly equate with the 'free choice' between men and women as sexual partners that Foucault identifies in the ancient Greek world, the belief 'that the same desire attached to anything that was desirable – boy or girl – subject to the condition that the appetite was nobler that inclined toward what was more beautiful or more honorable' (Foucault 1987: 188–92). Nevertheless, in Rochester's 'Song' it is the act that matters; no inference is being made about a particular sort of person who engages in the act. That would come later.

It is, of course, true that in Rochester's time sodomy was a capital crime. But its meaning was not restricted to sexual relations between men. In the early sixteenth century the word covered a variety of practices: it proscribed anal intercourse (with anyone), but also the use of a dildo or sex with animals. (Even today in those parts of the United States where sodomy laws remain on the statute books they typically include cunnilingus and fellatio and make no distinction between their practice by heterosexual and non-heterosexual persons.) Moreover, sodomy played a complicated role in the religious politics of the period. In Protestant England the Papacy was often identified with the corrupt biblical city of Sodom and hence was seen as a hotbed of vice, with buggery being defined as a peculiarly Italian habit (Cohen 1993: 103–6). In similar vein, Rochester's ribald poem 'Signior Dildo' (*c.* 1673) seems to have been occasioned by the controversial marriage of the heir presumptive to a Catholic princess from Italy, an event which the poet facetiously linked to the import of Italian dildoes into the country. The point, once again, is that the legal category of 'sodomy' did not correspond to the modern notion of 'homosexuality'.

If it is impossible to imagine a history of 'homosexuality' that is not primarily a history of our medical and legal categories and their impact upon us, what of same-sex passion? What kind of history might it have? This has been a productive, but at the same time an immensely difficult, question. Historians like Randolph Trumbach and Alan Bray have found evidence of what they see as 'sodomitical subcultures' coming into existence in major urban centres like London by the early eighteenth century. Trumbach, for example, has argued that 'a profound shift occurred in the conceptualization and practice of male homosexual behaviour' during this period, but sees this as part of a wider 'reorganization of gender identity' in which the differences between men and women started to become more sharply defined. In an argument that echoes Thomas Laqueur's account of the two-sex model, Trumbach claims that the majority of men now came to regard themselves as male 'because they felt attraction to women, and to women alone' (Trumbach 1987: 118). Not only did this 'gender revolution' undermine the older idea of the sodomite as someone who would engage in sex with boys *and* women, it also made sexual interest among men more dangerous than ever before. In London's post-Restoration theatre, for example, references to sodomy began to be suppressed and to portray unmanly fops on stage was to court legal and financial disaster (Senelick 1990). Notice that the word 'fop' has acquired a new meaning here: when Rochester writes of a 'rival fop' he is merely referring to someone whom he thinks is an insipid fool, but by the early eighteenth century the term has come to be associated with effeminacy and a male desire for the love of men (Wilmot 1994: 191). And it is worth adding that 'effeminacy' – a word that could variously mean 'tender', 'soft', 'gentle' or 'womanly' – only began to take on specifically sexual overtones around 1700. In Thomas Nashe's description of the defeat of the Anabaptist uprising in *The Unfortunate Traveller* (1594), for example, the mood of 'stern revenge' among the Imperial troops 'made them so eager [i.e. to slaughter their enemies] that their hands had no leisure to ask counsel of their effeminate eyes' – in other words, these men killed without mercy or compassion (Nashe 1972: 285).

Was the sodomite beginning to turn into the modern homosexual by 1700? In their discussion of 'sodomitical subcultures', both Trumbach and Bray emphasize the historical importance of the 'mollies' as an early example of what a collective same-sex lifestyle might look like. As one eighteenth-century observer put it, these were men who 'mimick all manner of Effeminacy . . . that they may tempt one another, by such immodest Freedoms, to commit those odious Beastialities, that ought for ever to be without a Name' (Ward 1756 [1709] : 265). Stories survive of their nightly meetings in a room in a tavern where they rapidly became renowned for their cross-dressing and elaborate rituals such as the simulation of childbirth and long sessions spent gossiping about their husbands and children.

Reading these descriptions today it is hard not to see the sexual underground of the mollies as the distant forerunners of the Harlem drag balls captured in Jennie Livingston's 1991 documentary film *Paris Is Burning*, a portrait of a self-subsistent enclave whose members compulsively mime and parody the conventions of the straight world around them. The molly sounds like a new kind of identity, a step into the future; it was, writes Alan Bray, 'a broader word' than the older term 'sodomite' and was not necessarily 'intrinsically sexual at all' (Bray 1995 [1982]: 103). But unfortunately our information about these men is extremely sketchy, drawing heavily on court records and other unsympathetic sources. Edward Ward's *A Compleat and Humorous Account Of All the Remarkable Clubs and Societies in the City of London and Westminster* cited above was clearly written to divert and entertain its readers, and alongside the account of the 'Men who chuse this backward Way' are tales of the 'Club of Ugly Faces' and the 'Farting Club'. And what is one to make of the doggerel which ends this section?

> But *Sodomites* their Wives forsake
> Unmanly Liberties to take;
> And fall in Love with one another
> As if no Woman was their Mother.
>   (Ward 1756: 268–9)

Is this evidence that the 'molly' was not so very different from the sodomite after all; or is it merely a piece of invective or perhaps a cheap jibe? Conspicuously absent here are any first-hand accounts of how the mollies viewed themselves, or how they regarded their own activities.

Nevertheless, the idea that in 'the Mollies Club' we see the crucible of modern gay culture remains a tantalizing, if uncertain, possibility. Historians continue to disagree as to whether it makes sense to talk about well-established sodomitical subcultures in eighteenth-century London. The picture only starts to become clearer as we move towards the present. Once again, the coining of new words or new usages offers important clues: according to the *Oxford English Dictionary*, for instance, 'drag' (in the sense of men dressing up in female attire) and 'lesbian' can both be traced back to the 1870s and obviously pre-date the Wilde trials, while another cluster of explicit and/or derogatory terms like 'queen', 'queer', 'pansy' and 'homo' seems to enter the language in the 1920s. These popular linguistic shifts imply that modern gay or lesbian identities did not emerge solely in a space created for them by medical and legal judgments, as the first volume of Foucault's *History of Sexuality* tends to suggest; rather, they were the product of a complex interaction between familiar, subcultural values and practices on the one hand and attempts at control by the state and the professions on the other.

By far the fullest and most detailed cultural history of gay urban life is George Chauncey's pathbreaking book *Gay New York* (1994) which covers the period from 1890 to the outbreak of the Second World War. Combining personal recollections and private diaries with official archival sources, Chauncey not only charts the changing fortunes of the city's gay male communities, but also examines the interface – the conflict and the mutuality – between the nation's 'gay capital' and the 'normal' or 'straight' world. Here different languages, vernacular and regulatory, overlapped and collided. To the police, doctors and anti-vice campaigners gay men were 'inverts', 'perverts', 'degenerates' or sometimes 'homosexuals' or 'homosexualists', while the men would identify themselves variously as 'faggots', 'fairies' or 'queens', words that had many more subtle inflections than when they were used homophobically as insults or as terms of abuse. For these slang words were highly mobile: 'faggot' (later corrupted to 'fag') seems, for example, to have originally circulated among African-American gay men before it was taken up by whites.

However, as Chauncey notes, by the 1910s and 1920s the word most often chosen to indicate that they belonged to 'a distinct category of men' who were sexually interested in other men (though not necessarily adopting or approving a blatantly 'effeminate manner') was *queer* (Chauncey 1994: 15–16). In the 1940s the preferred term had become 'gay', but by then the world had begun to change and the cultural climate had become more inhospitable to lesbians and male homosexuals. 'Gay' was not really an equivalent to 'queer': it was at once a more guarded signifier of belonging, a word that was frequently used with caution – outsiders would not at first have understood what 'having a gay time' or being in a 'gay bar' meant. Yet it was also paradoxically a more inclusive word, sometimes referring specifically to those ostentatious styles of dress and deportment that the word 'queer' had tended to preclude. The next section considers some of the reasons behind this change and looks at two individuals who tried sometimes to confront and sometimes to side-step the homophobic ethos of the 1950s and early 1960s: James Baldwin (1925–87) and Andy Warhol (1928–87).

IN AND OUT OF THE CLOSET

Gay New York is essentially a work of retrieval. In it Chauncey seeks to recover the lives and lifestyles of those gay men whose past has been hidden from history, whose culture has been forgotten and in part erased or distorted. One of Chauncey's central claims is that the common idea that same-sex desire was necessarily a solitary, secretive longing that could not be given public expression is a myth, and a relatively recent myth at that. True, queer behaviour was parodied, proscribed and policed, but, in New York in the early decades of the twentieth century at least, it was by no means confined to the closet. The open portrayal of gay men and women on stage in such Broadway plays as Edouard Bournet's *The Captive* or in comedienne Mae West's work is just one sign of the extent to which homosexuality had come to be taken for granted in the city, leading the state legislature to pass the repressive 'Padlock Law' in 1927 in an attempt to outlaw this kind of subject matter, although allusions to homosexuality continued to appear in Broadway productions such as Noël Coward's *Design for Living* (1933). During these years drag balls were hugely popular events in New York and were held at major public venues like Madison Square Gardens, Harlem's Savoy Ballroom or the Astor Hotel. Indeed, anti-gay measures like the Padlock Law were deliberately intended to roll back the increasing visibility of the gay subculture, particularly by targeting the social milieux where gay men and women socialized. After 1933, for instance, it became an offence for gays to gather in licensed public places like clubs or restaurants.

As a result of this legislative onslaught, homosexuals were forced to go underground, to cut themselves off from the mainstream of city life, and to exercise much more care and discretion about the ways in which they presented themselves – in other words, to enter the closet. The growing use of the term 'gay' as the most common synonym for 'homosexual' was related to this new experience of segregation for it presupposed a rigidly divided world in which heterosexuality was the norm. In the space of a generation 'the lines had been drawn between the heterosexual and the homosexual so sharply and publicly that men were no longer able to participate in a homosexual encounter without suspecting it meant (to the outside world, and to themselves) that they were gay' (Chauncey 1994: 22). This had not been true of 'queers' or 'fairies': these were contrasting, sometimes transitory, gendered personae or styles based upon an individual's sense of himself as masculine or feminine rather than his choice of sexual partner.

Men who regarded themselves as queer could be intensely hostile to the more effeminate fairies. William S. Burroughs' early writings are a good example of this frequently aggressive attitude. In a 1955 letter to Allen Ginsberg and Jack Kerouac, for instance, Burroughs condemns those he calls 'complete swish fairies' and wishes to see them all dead, not merely because they are 'traitors to the cause of queerness, but for selling out the human race to the forces of negation and death' (Burroughs 1994: 298). Burroughs' murderous invective shows not only the continuing survival of the older gendered vocabulary alongside the new, more capacious rhetoric of gayness; it also indicates some of the tensions arising from the policing of the closet and a fear and hatred of those self-endangering forms of public display that grated against the boundaries of heterosexual normalcy. As an antidote to the repressiveness of the American scene, Burroughs tended to idealize the sexual liaisons that occurred on his visits to South America and North Africa, applauding the uninhibited ease with which the 'average, *non-queer* Peruvian boy' will 'go to bed with another male' and underplaying the cash basis of this type of sexual tourism (Burroughs 1994: 176).

Many of the gay men interviewed in *Gay New York* regarded the 1930s as a relatively unthreatening time when compared to the virulent campaigns against them in the aftermath of the Second World War. The crude homophobia featured in bestselling crime novelist Mickey Spillane's work, ranging from the punches and cold water thrown at gay men in *I, the Jury* (1947) to the depiction of transvestism as the most monstrous symbol of evil in *Vengeance Is Mine!* (1950), is symptomatic of the worst literary excesses of this period. But other texts from the 1950s provide more complex manifestations of this homophobic impulse. Robert J. Corber has recently shown how the films of Alfred Hitchcock echoed contemporary panics about the threat to national security arising from the presence of gay employees in the US federal government. In his 1951 film adaptation of the novel *Strangers on a Train*, for instance, Hitchcock significantly moves the narrative's locale from New York and Connecticut to Washington DC and, by portraying the criminal Charles Bruno as a homosexual, dramatizes the widespread fear that straight men who became entangled with gays were likely to find themselves the victims of blackmail. Moreover, Bruno's pathology is identified through one of the major medical explanations of same-sex eroticism prevalent in the 1950s: his homosexuality is a form of 'arrested sexual development', 'an unresolved Oedipus complex' stemming from an emotional over-dependence on his mother (Corber 1993: 72). In one shot we even see her manicuring Bruno's nails.

From the other side of the homophobic divide, so to speak, perhaps the most troubled and troubling American representation of homosexuality from within the closet is James Baldwin's *Giovanni's Room* (1957). Despite the success of his first novel *Go Tell It on the Mountain* (1953), *Giovanni's Room* was turned down by Baldwin's American publishers because they were afraid that the book would make him known as a black homosexual writer. It was only taken up in the United States after having initially appeared in England. *Giovanni's Room* is the story of a young white man's struggle with his desires as he looks back at the devastating consequences his irresolution has had upon the other people in his life. At first the narrator implies that it is the sheer complexity, the disordered multiplicity of his passions that leads him to betray himself and the men and women who have loved him. 'I am too various to be trusted,' David confesses by way of explaining why 'the great difficulty is to say Yes to life' (Baldwin 1990: 11). But more is at stake than a failure of commitment, for David's self-interrogation takes place under the shadow of his lover Giovanni's impending execution for murder.

In a crucial passage, David queasily describes the gay bar, 'a noisy, crowded, ill-lit sort of tunnel', where he was introduced to Giovanni. Or, more precisely, he describes its clientele, '*les folles*':

> Occasionally one would swoop in, quite late in the evening, to convey the news that he – but they always called each other 'she' – had just spent time with a celebrated movie star, or boxer. Then all of the others closed in on this newcomer and they looked like a peacock garden and sounded like a barnyard. I always found it difficult to believe that they ever went to bed with anybody for a man who wanted a woman would certainly have rather had a real one and a man who wanted a man would certainly not want one of *them*. Perhaps, indeed, that was why they screamed so loud.

(Baldwin 1990: 29–30)

Superficially, this description resembles the anathematization of the 'fairy' that we found in Burroughs' early writings and elsewhere in the novel David expresses disgust at the 'fairy's mannerisms' that he sees Giovanni starting to adopt (139). But David's desire lacks any point of lasting affirmation and his denial, condemned by Giovanni as an inability to love, is the product of a complex set of displacements, terrors that he scarcely knows how to articulate. For, on the one hand, David both hates and fears women, often remembering or positioning himself as a vulnerable small boy in their presence; while, on the other, the love that he can never fully acknowledge is a love of black men: the brown-skinned Joey who was his first lover or the 'insolent and dark and leonine' southern Italian barman Giovanni (31). This gives a special tone to Giovanni's final accusation that David cannot embrace the physicality of the other, that he wants 'to despise Giovanni because he is not afraid of the stink of love' (134). And so, at the end of the novel, when David tries to visualize Giovanni's murder of the bar-owner ('a silly old queen') who has dismissed him, the scenario that David imagines is coloured by his own curiously involuted homophobia. The 'blackness' that 'comes and goes' before Giovanni's eyes brings to mind the 'cavern' that opens in David's mind, 'black, full of rumor, suggestion, of half-heard, half-forgotten, half-understood stories, full of dirty words', after he has slept with Joey (14, 146–7). Lucidity and self-hatred go hand in hand here: the more David sees, the more he is trapped by a revulsion at his own deepest desires.

Baldwin's own views about homosexuality provide an instructive counterpoint to *Giovanni's Room*. In an early essay on the gay French author André Gide written in 1954, for example, Baldwin sought both to transcend the reduction of homosexuality to mere sexual behaviour, whether natural or not, *and* at the same time to insist that the division of the world into 'two sexes' was an unavoidable fact with which everyone must in some way come to terms, 'no matter what demons drive them'. What Baldwin saw as the compulsive promiscuity of gay life ('a meaningless round of conquests') ultimately seemed to him to be as dehumanizing as the superficial commodification of sexuality manifested by 'the breasts of Holly-wood glamour girls and the mindless grunting and swaggering of Hollywood he-men' – not forgetting 'the heroes of Mickey Spillane'. For Baldwin humankind's greatest need was 'to arrive at something higher than a natural state', to strive towards the 'genuine human involvement' of love and friendship that must necessarily include 'communion between the sexes' (Baldwin 1985: 101–5).

Some thirty years later he was to push these ideas in a still more radical direction by arguing that our capacity for love had been wholly distorted by the false 'American ideal of masculinity' with its dead-end oppositions: 'punks and studs, tough guys and softies, butch and faggot, black and white'. To be called a faggot was to be 'told simply that you had no balls'. Against this divisive and destructive logic, Baldwin argued that 'we are all androgynous' since 'each of us, helplessly and forever, contains the other – male in female, female in male, white in black and black in white' (Baldwin 1985: 677–90). This formulation should not be confused with the old nineteenth-century notion of homosexuality as a 'third' or 'intermediate sex' in which male and female elements commingle in the same person. Far from being a special case, Baldwin identifies androgyny with the human condition *per se*. Indeed his essay, originally entitled 'Freaks and the American Ideal of Manhood' (and subsequently re-named 'Here Be Dragons') was partly inspired by the gender-bending personae of performers like Boy George and Michael Jackson, figures who might be thought to play upon or externalize what is for Baldwin our unrecognized inner being. But the danger in Baldwin's endeavour to deconstruct the category of homosexuality is that the very possibility, not to mention the value, of a specifically gay identity can all too easily be elided. Elsewhere Baldwin did speak of the need to bear 'a kind of witness' to 'that phenomenon we call gay'; yet, as Kendall Thomas has shown, this insistence has often been ignored in some of the attempts selectively to lay claim to Baldwin's cultural and political legacy since his death in 1987 (Thomas 1996: 56).

To move to the creative world of Andy Warhol is at once to enter a lighter, airier, apparently less serious domain, an *oeuvre* that seems deliberately to eschew hard moral judgements and to concern itself instead with style and pleasure. In that sense Warhol's work is frequently closer in spirit to that of Boy George and Michael Jackson and indeed the Factory, Warhol's New York production base in the 1960s, was a place that brought members of the worlds of art and pop together. To be sure, there was always a puzzling and much darker side to Warhol's art: controversy still surrounds the possible meanings of his early *Disaster Series* from around 1963 – multiple images of electric chairs, race riots and car wrecks – and Warhol's bleak 1981 series of *Self-Portraits* in drag remain among his most haunting and disturbing representations. But certainly in the 1960s Warhol's name also quickly became a synonym for everything that was daring, outrageous, yet also fun.

One of the key terms deployed to make sense of Warhol's art during this period was 'Camp'. Like 'drag' or 'queer', the word 'camp' has a primarily gay provenance. At the turn of the nineteenth century it originally meant affected, theatrical or effeminate, and to say 'how very camp he is' was effectively to identify someone as a homosexual. While it retained this core meaning, by the 1960s the use of the term had broadened (and acquired a capital 'C') to signify a distinctive set of cultural preferences or a kind of taste, a highly aestheticized way of looking at things. Probably the single most influential account of this sensibility appeared in Susan Sontag's 1964 'Notes on "Camp"', an attempt to pin down some of the more elusive features of a contradictory phenomenon that seemed to resist systematic analysis. Sontag associated Camp with the artificial, the extravagant, the frivolous, the stylish, the playful. But the inherent complexity of these attributes means that none of them can be allowed to stand without qualification. For example, to say that Camp is typically 'anti-serious' is only half-true; rather, the serious element in Camp is always punctured by its own excesses; hence the paradox that in Camp 'one can be serious about the frivolous, frivolous about the serious' (Sontag 1966: 288).

While Sontag suggests that 'homosexuals, by and large, constitute the vanguard – and the most articulate audience – of Camp', she denies that there is any necessary or intrinsic connection, on the grounds that 'if homosexuals hadn't more or less invented Camp, someone else would' (291). Yet one of her own most acute insights tells against this assertion. Early in her article, Sontag observes that Camp recognizes an 'unacknowledged truth of taste: the most refined form of sexual attractiveness (as well as the most refined form of sexual pleasure) consists in going against the grain of one's sex'. This is why the figure of the androgyne is so highly prized by the Camp sensibility, but also why there is 'a relish for the exaggeration of sexual characteristics and personality mannerisms': the overblown he-men and sex-goddesses of the Hollywood film industry. In other words, Camp refuses to take at anything other than face value precisely those figures whom James Baldwin took to be symptoms of the modern American malaise. In Camp gender differences increasingly approximate to the condition of display or masquerade.

Instead of looking for the inner truth behind appearances, 'Camp sees everything in quotation marks . . . not a woman, but a "woman"' (279–80).

Warhol's preoccupation with fashion, image and glamour can be traced back to his childhood when he collected signed photographs of film stars and celebrities. But it was given added impetus during his formative, post-college years as a commercial artist hired by luxury department stores like New York's Bonwit Teller and was then carried over into his paintings, films and, later, his journalism. Hence, among many others, the potentially unlimited repetition of silkscreen images of Marilyn Monroe (*Marilyn Monroe [Twenty Times]*,1961 or *Twenty-Five Coloured Marilyns*, 1962) and Elvis Presley (*Elvis 1*, 1964). As in Warhol's famous canvases of multiple Campbell Soup cans there is a provocative mixing of genres in these works. Publicity stills, product design and news photographs were absorbed into painting in such a way as to muddy the usually clear-cut distinction between consumer culture and high art. Moreover Warhol's preferred techniques had the effect of foregrounding the constructed quality of the image: starting from photographs that he would first carefully modify or enhance, Warhol would prepare a coloured image on canvas and then overlay this with a silkscreen print that reproduced the details from the original photo; but the lack of perfect fit between canvas and silkscreen created a discordant sensation, as though the blocks of paint had been misapplied. Here gendered identity looks as if it has been poorly simulated or hastily assembled, an impression that is heightened by the garish and metallic colours Warhol used. In a sense, artifice and desire are being put into contradiction in the Marilyn Monroe portraits. 'Marilyn's lips weren't kissable,' Warhol once observed, 'but they were very photographable' (Warhol 1977: 54).

In the popular magazines of the period, the vocabulary of Camp allowed columnists to refer discreetly to Warhol's gayness, or at least to label him as unconventional or eccentric in his cultural tastes. Reviewing his latest New York exhibition in December 1964, for example, *Newsweek* dubbed Warhol 'Saint Andrew' and placed him at the head of a 'new hip world of blurred genders' (quoted in Whiting 1997: 183). But this was just the beginning. As Warhol moved into film-making between 1968 and 1972, the gay content of his work became more overt (or one might say that his work became more Camp): his 1972 movie *Women in Revolt!* starred three transvestites in the lead roles playing 'women in varying degrees of "liberation"' and in 1975 Warhol produced a series of portraits of black and Hispanic drag queens called *Ladies and Gentlemen* (Warhol 1977: 54). Drag queens occupied an important place in Warhol's imagination:

> Among other things, drag queens are living testimony to the way women used to want to be, the way some people still want them to be, and the way some women still actually want to be. Drags are ambulatory archives of ideal moviestar womanhood. They perform a documentary service, usually consecrating their lives to keeping the glittering alternative alive and available for (not-too-close) inspection.
>
> (Warhol 1977: 54)

Warhol was enormously impressed by the 'very hard work' required of 'boys who spend their lives trying to be complete girls', work which he saw as centrally concerned with the imitation of a fantasy – hence his droll one-liner on the paradoxes of desire: 'I always run into strong women who are looking for weak men to dominate them' (54–6). Nevertheless, according to the logic of Warhol's position, drag queens are by no means an indispensable part of the show. For if drag queens were sometimes preferable to 'the real girls we knew' who 'couldn't seem to get excited about anything', because 'the drag queens could get excited about anything', once 'the girls seem to be getting their energy back', then 'real ones' could be brought back into his movies again (Warhol 1977: 55). On this view, gender is very much a question of performance and gendered identity is largely a matter of whoever performs best, of who has the most style.

In her 'Notes on "Camp"', Sontag argues that the 'flamboyant mannerisms' associated with Camp are 'gestures full of duplicity', operating on two levels: 'a witty meaning for cognoscenti and another, more impersonal, for outsiders' (Sontag 1966: 281). Put like this, Camp can be read as an ostentatious strategy of dissimulation or concealment, a way of signalling that one is 'passing' among straights while simultaneously having the last laugh on them. But Warhol's use of Camp was marked by a tendency to dissolve identity into a deceptive play of surfaces, cultivating a blank or disengaged persona that made the very idea of a self more elusive than ever. Reflecting on his visit to the Paris fashion shows in 1981, Warhol noted that 'all the really straight-looking [male] models are gay, and all the really gay-looking models are straight' and, after discussing this with a friend, decided to 'start telling people that despite how we look and talk, that we're not gay. Because then they don't know what to do with you' (Warhol 1989: 369). In Warhol's hands Camp becomes more than an insider's joke, it becomes an elaborate double bind in which to trap the unwary by both publicly flaunting and impassively denying his gayness at one and the same time.

QUEER SENSIBILITIES, QUEER THEORY

Just as Warhol's deadpan swishiness helped to open up new aesthetic possibilities for Camp as a cultural practice, so 'queer' is also a term that has been virtually reinvented by gay critics and gay activists in recent years. Roughly speaking, 'queer' seems to have passed through three main phases. When the word first came into use in the United States it was not a mark of obloquy or disdain; as one respondent who had been part of New York's gay world in the 1920s told George Chauncey: 'It wasn't like kike or nigger. . . . It just meant you were different' (Chauncey 1994: 101). In deliberate contrast with the fairy, to identify oneself as queer tended to indicate a quietly controlled, 'manly' demeanour and a desire for other queer, or perhaps straight men. According to Chauncey's evidence, the queer/fairy opposition reflected the social class backgrounds from which these gendered styles typically originated. From the middle-class standpoint of the average queer man, the fairy represented a tasteless, undignified, and above all lower-class mode of self-presentation that brought same-sex relationships into disrepute. But, on the other hand, class was not always a source of antagonism; for many men class differences could also stimulate desire, E.M. Forster's wish 'to love a strong young man of the lower classes and be loved by him and even hurt by him' (and then to write 'respectable novels') being a famous case in point (Forster 1989: 16).

By the 1940s queer had ceased to be a relatively neutral term. Thus, when his publisher wanted to call his second book *Fag* instead of *Queer*, William Burroughs was appalled. 'I don't mind being called queer,' he wrote to Allen Ginsberg, 'but I'll see him castrated before I'll be called a Fag' (Burroughs 1994: 119). The year was 1952 and Burroughs' response reflects not only the habits of mind of an earlier generation (not to mention his privileged upbringing), but it also carries the clear implication that being called 'queer' was now something that one might well mind. For the letters repeatedly show how powerful a psychological and cultural norm hetero-sexuality had become. In the early 1950s Ginsberg was so distressed by his desire for men that he was seeing a psychoanalyst to help him 'to get over being queer' (85). So it is crucial to Burroughs' defence of calling himself queer that sleeping with women does not make him heterosexual: 'Laying a woman, so far as I am concerned is O.K. if I can't score for a boy. But laying one woman or a thousand merely *emphasizes* the fact that a woman is not what I want' (88).

Revealingly, 'queer' also had another meaning in the 1950s. When David in *Giovanni's Room* tells one of his male companions in a gay bar that 'I'm sort of queer for girls myself' he is turning the word against a would-be lover and also using the word in a somewhat different sense to indicate both the source and the intensity of his desire. To say that you were 'queer for someone' meant that you felt passionately about that person, that you were head over heels in love with them, and was a phrase that could be used by men and women. In his autobiographical novel *Junkie* (1953), William Burroughs writes of 'queer joints' (gay bars) and the wealthy 'international queer set', but just a few pages later the word's inflection changes when a prostitute named Mary says of her boyfriend 'I'm queer for Jack' – though she subsequently tells the narrator that she is mostly attracted to women (Burroughs 1966: 9, 25).

Mad for a man, yet preferring women: this figure of a passion that is aberrant precisely because it is uncontainable and uncontrollable, carries over into queer's latest incarnation, a phase in which queer becomes a signifier of attitude, of a refusal to accept conventional sexual and gendered categories, of a defiant desire *beyond* the regular confines of 'heteronormativity'. According to Eve Kosofsky Sedgwick's marvellously eloquent and much-quoted definition:

> Queer can refer to: the open mesh of possibilities, gaps, overlaps, dissonances and resonances, lapses and excesses of meaning when the constituent elements of anyone's gender, of anyone's sexuality aren't made (or *can't* be made) to signify monolithically.
>
> (Sedgwick 1993: 8)

This is desire in all its incalculable, inconvenient unboundedness and its corollary is, in Judith Butler's celebrated phrase, gender 'as *trouble*' (Butler 1990: ix).

We should be careful therefore not to let the polymorphous accents of this more permissive version of queer eradicate either its radical edge or its unapologetically militant history. As Sedgwick herself adds in a crucial qualification, 'to disavow' the specific links between queerness and homosexuality or 'to displace' such associations 'from the term's definitional centre' would be to rob it of its emancipatory potential (Sedgwick 1993: 8). For the first strategic redeployment of the word came in 1990 with the founding of the activist group Queer Nation in New York, a move that grew directly out of political work on behalf of people suffering from AIDS. By staging a series of daring affronts to contemporary civic culture, Queer Nation has sought to force the general public to face up to some of the unexamined lines of symbolic demarcation between gays and straights in everyday life. Queer Nation's 'visibility actions' have combined the sardonic and the provocative, the theatrical and the confrontational to create vivid, highly charged moments of recognition: hence the surprise occupations of exclusively heterosexual bars or the organized 'kiss-ins' at city plazas and shopping malls, tactics designed to challenge the limits of the straight imagination. While these sorts of happenings are in one sense celebratory manifestations of a gay presence, they involve more than a simple transvaluation of 'queer' that turns it from a negative into a positive term. The popular slogan 'We're here! We're queer! Get used to it!' points a critical finger at existing institutions and articulates a far-reaching demand for change.

What difference might queer theory make to literary or cultural criticism? These are still early days, but on the whole queer critics have been more interested in developing new modes of interpreting literary texts or in asking new questions of them, than in constructing a gay and lesbian counter-canon of great books, though it goes without saying that queer theorists certainly have strong views on what is worthy of their readers' attention. The results have been extremely varied: 'queer readings' of such major writers as James Joyce and Henry James can be found side by side with discussions of less established figures like Vita Sackville-West, Audre Lorde or Neil Bartlett.

A sample from the recent critical history of Djuna Barnes' 1936 novel *Nightwood* provides an instructive example of some of the ways in which queer theory departs from earlier approaches. Barnes was rated highly by her peers – T.S. Eliot and James Joyce both championed her work – yet her writings stand at an odd angle to canonical modernism. And *Nightwood*, a book widely acknowledged as Barnes's *chef-d'oeuvre*, has proved particularly difficult to place. Not surprisingly, it resists easy summary. The novel begins with the birth of Felix Volkbein in Vienna at the turn of the century, but then swiftly backtracks into a family genealogy that shows the pomp of the Volkbein coat of arms to be nothing more than the pretence of a Jewish parvenu. As a grown man, Felix cultivates the eccentric company of circus artists and theatre players who live on the fringes of European high society and through whom he meets his young wife, Robin Vote. But no sooner are they married than the novel swerves off into what will become its central narrative, the story of Robin's intense affair with the circus publicity agent Nora Flood, a relationship that is violently disrupted when Robin is seduced by the voracious Jenny Petherbridge. Much of the rest of the book chronicles Nora's agonized and inconclusive efforts to repair this loss.

But to outline the plot as if it were a simple sequence of events is to seriously misrepresent the true nature of Barnes's achievement. For one thing, *Nightwood* is, above all else, a novel of talk, a book that dazzles through its wonderfully inventive use of language, its obsessive exploration of mood and metaphysics, rather than through its analysis of character and situation. Thus it is entirely appropriate that Dr Matthew O'Connor, arguably the most extraordinary figure in the book, speaks almost entirely in lofty yet racy monologues, even when he is engaged in conversation. And so dense and ornate is the verbal texture of the novel that the puzzling question of *what* is being said often pushes a character's motives for speaking into the background.

If the main relationships in the book are between women, doesn't it make sense to read *Nightwood* as 'a narrative of lesbian desire and power' (Allen 1993: 181)? Especially, one might add, since the novel relies heavily for its setting upon the Parisian gay community in which Barnes herself lived and worked during the 1920s. Carolyn Allen succeeds brilliantly in tracing the 'complex dynamics between lesbian subjects', in revealing the forces that draw Nora and Robin together and wrench them apart (180). But the problem with this optic is that it drastically reduces the scope of the book, sidelining the carnivalesque world of misfits and outsiders whose 'ranting' and 'roaring' provide *Nightwood*'s true ambience, irrespective of place. The antinomianism of this strangely hybrid 'crew' is well illustrated by the promiscuous gathering at Nora's '"paupers" salon' outside New York, a mecca 'for poets, radicals, beggars, artists, and people in love; for Catholics, Protestants, Brahmins, dabblers in black magic and medicine', as well as the performers from the Denckman circus (Barnes 1961: 50). Fittingly, Nora was 'brought . . . into the world' by none other than the transvestite Dr O'Connor, who subsequently fulfils the combined functions of Nora's phallic mother and father confessor, her priest and analyst (49). Nevertheless, it is important for Allen's reading to emphasize that Dr O'Connor's ministrations must finally be seen to be defeated by Nora in order for lesbian passion to retain its integrity in the face of an unhappy ending.

O'Connor has also been described as a 'witch doctor or medicine man', an appellation which seems to position him as *Nightwood*'s principal shaman or magician. According to Sandra Gilbert, O'Connor's verbal magic bespeaks 'the androgynous wholeness and holiness of prehistory' that is ultimately invoked by the text in an attempt to escape from 'the dis-order and dis-ease of gender'. There is, she argues, a sharp distinction to be made between the use of transvestism in the work of male modernists like Joyce and Eliot as compared to that of Djuna Barnes or Virginia Woolf. In the Nighttown episode of Joyce's *Ulysses*, for example, when the 'massive' brothelkeeper Bella Cohen makes Leopold Bloom 'shed [his] male garments' for a 'punishment frock' and 'don the shot silk luxuriously rustling over head and shoulders', this ritualized unmanning is in fact a prelude to the restoration of Bloom's 'proximate erection' (Joyce 1964 [1922]: 647, 867). But in *Nightwood* – read by Gilbert as 'a revisionary response' to Joyce's Nighttown – the inconstancy of gendered identities produces 'a symbolic chaos' whose sign is a ubiquitous androgyny which precludes any return to patriarchal certainties. And it is this 'wild reality beyond gender' that explains *Nightwood*'s strong affinity for the mythic and the transcendental.

At the novel's close Nora follows Robin to a remote country chapel where her former lover gets down on her hands and knees and starts to behave like an animal. In Gilbert's view this curious final scene has an almost mystical significance, for 'Robin actually does become a kind of sacred Dog, a reversed God (or Goddess) of the third sex, parodically barking before a conventional statuette of the Madonna' (Gilbert 1980: 413–15).

Each of these readings goes a long way towards illuminating the difficulties inherent in what is often an opaque and obscure text. But, if Allen's specific focus on lesbian desire might be thought to leave too much out, Gilbert's more inclusive claim that the novel finds its fulfilment in an all-encompassing androgyny could be said to overlook the extent to which *Nightwood* perversely refuses any such easy resolution. When Dr O'Connor suddenly exclaims 'It's my mother without argument I want!' (Barnes 1961: 149) or when the anguished Nora cries out 'I can't live without my heart!' (156), both characters are giving voice to their sense of desolation and incompleteness by naming the lost object that they cannot have. One of the many virtues of Joseph A. Boone's excellent queer reading of *Nightwood* in his book *Libidinal Currents* (1998) is its alertness to precisely these moments of frustration and terror, its recognition that Barnes eschews any conclusion 'that would impose final meaning on the queer desires of the sexually disenfranchised that this text so defiantly champions' (Boone 1998: 242).

Though in no way seeking to diminish the force of lesbianism's presence in *Nightwood*, Boone argues that the adoption of a queer perspective may have a special relevance here. In the first place, the world of the novel 'transcends the limits of the hetero/homo divide' so completely that even those characters like Felix Volkbein who yearn for respectability and security find themselves utterly undone (Boone 1998: 234). Indeed, the ordinary categories of experience are repeatedly stretched to breaking-point: O'Connor, the suspect doctor, is simultaneously 'a boy', 'the bearded lady' and 'the last woman left in this world', while Robin is 'a wild thing caught in a woman's skin, monstrously alone, monstrously vain' (Barnes 1961: 100, 146). As these examples suggest, the term 'queer' can also be applied to Barnes's language and style since her words tend to operate 'on the level of surface, sound, and combination with other word-images, rather than serving as an index of rational meaning'. Moreover, Boone sees a close parallel between the condition of 'permanent alienation' in which 'the narrative's queer subjects' live as social and sexual outcasts and the way in which the constant use of oxymorons, discordant metaphors and almost surreal juxtapositions in the novel tends to exile words from their established meanings (Boone 1998: 238–9). In its radical will to experiment, to re-make language, *Nightwood* surely qualifies as one of the founding texts of what we might now call 'queer modernism'.

Barnes's persistent denaturalization of language, her preference for the artificial and the baroque, has an important effect upon characterization for which the circus or the theatre provides the most apposite image. Felix Volkbein, 'the wandering Jew', is a man in search of the means of his own self-transformation and what draws him to these actresses, acrobats and sword-swallowers is their love of 'pageantry', 'their splendid and reeking falsification' (Barnes 1961: 7, 11). Just as language runs away with (and from) the novel's characters, so any hope that we might gain access to their inner thoughts is seriously undermined:

> Rather, the intensely psychodramatic material of *Nightwood* is projected outward onto the narrative plane, rendering interiority a textual theatre where sexuality and identity are self-consciously staged and performed. Even those narrative moments that the reader may think provide glimpses into the inner depths of these characters ultimately reveal that what lies 'behind the surface' is pure theatre, a facade of surface upon surface that underscores the secondariness and estrangement in all representation.
>
> (Boone 1998: 248).

There is something close to the spirit of Camp in this stress upon performance and superficiality and in *Nightwood* it occurs in the most unlikely places. When Dr O'Connor is called to Robin Vote's hotel bedroom after she has fainted his first act is lightly to use her perfume, powder and lipstick to make himself up while Felix voyeuristically looks on from behind a jungle of potted palms. What promised to be a privileged moment of insight has turned into a carefully orchestrated spectacle, another reminder that 'the performative play of surfaces is *all* we ever get' (Boone 1998: 249). Robin's emergence from her trance is no less theatrical, her voice adopting 'the pitch of one enchanted with the gift of postponed abandon', or of 'the actor who, in the soft usury of his speech, withholds a vocabulary until the profitable moment when he shall be facing his audience'. Barnes's queer sensibility brings form and content into near perfect alignment in *Nightwood*, 'as an image and its reflection in a lake seem parted only by the hesitation in the hour' (Barnes 1961: 38).

'ANTICOMMUNITARIAN IMPULSES'

Historically, as *Nightwood* amply confirms, both modernism and same-sex passion have relied upon the twentieth-century metropolis as a place sufficiently large and diverse to enable them to survive, and eventually to flourish. But this link between sexual dissidence and urban geography can be found throughout gay and lesbian writing and not only in its modernist forms. Thus in Radclyffe Hall's distinctly non-modernist lesbian novel *The Well of Loneliness* (1928) it is in Paris that Stephen Gordon ultimately makes her home when she has been rejected by her mother Lady Anna and it is there that she most fully realizes her vocation as a writer. The novel requires that Stephen cannot find personal happiness since her tragic fate is to embody and articulate the crippling burden of social exclusion and denial that lesbians must bear, to use her literary gifts on behalf of the sexual pariah. Nevertheless, *The Well of Loneliness* does vouchsafe at least one positive glimpse of an alternative future via the gregarious and unbowed figure of Valerie Seymour, famed for her celebrated Parisian salon, who cheerfully predicts that Nature will soon redress the lesbian's minority status by bringing 'inverts' into the world in ever increasing numbers.

Despite their evident stylistic differences, *The Well of Loneliness* and *Nightwood* have each been read as flawed anticipations of a new kind of community in process. As we have seen, Boone is careful to note the ways in which Barnes deliberately seeks to estrange her readers from the text, refusing them any comfortable points of identification in *Nightwood*'s crepuscular narrative. Yet, at the same time, he argues that Barnes's 'perverse depiction of an entire universe of outcasts banded in solidarity under the sign of inversion' is precisely what aligns the novel with 'contemporary idioms of queer world-making' (Boone 1998: 235). The key word in this sentence is of course 'solidarity', with its communal overtones of belonging, companionship and self-sacrifice.

This line of argument has recently come under sustained attack from Leo Bersani in his book *Homos* (1995), a polemic directed against some of the most cherished assumptions within gay and lesbian studies, including queer theory. Bersani suggests that there is a profound ambivalence about what it currently means to be gay, a doubt as to whether it is possible (or even justifiable) to speak any longer of a specifically gay identity. The call for social justice – the demand that gays or lesbians should be treated no differently than anyone else – might be said to have the aggregate effect of making them the same as everyone else, of reducing their cultural visibility or distinctiveness as a group by assimilating them into the general (straight) population. Or again, some commentators have questioned whether one's choice of sexual partner should be regarded as the single most important index of who one is. In the words of Judith Butler's forceful disclaimer:

> The prospect of *being* anything, even for pay, has always produced in me a certain anxiety, for 'to be' gay, 'to be' lesbian seems to be

more than a simple injunction to become who or what I already am. And in no way does it settle the anxiety for me to say that this is 'part' of what I am. To write or speak *as a lesbian* appears a paradoxical appearance of this 'I,' one which feels neither true nor false. For it is a production, usually in response to a request, to come out or write in the name of an identity which, once produced, sometimes functions as a politically efficacious phantasm. I'm not at ease with 'lesbian theories, gay theories,' for as I've argued elsewhere, identity categories tend to be instruments of regulatory regimes, whether as the normalizing categories of oppressive structures or as the rallying points for a liberatory contestation of that very oppression. This is not to say that I will not appear at political occasions under the sign of lesbian, but that I would like to have it permanently unclear what precisely that sign signifies.

(Butler 1991: 13–14)

The attractions of this position are considerable: it invites one to break free from the stigmatizing logic of gender differences, to stop thinking of one's gender as some sort of fixed core or essence. Yet to refuse to be recognized as gay or lesbian is to abandon, or as Bersani puts it, to 'de-gay' gayness itself. Worse still, in practice it helps to make the homophobic dream become a reality by bringing about 'the elimination of gays' (Bersani 1995: 5).

What alternative does Bersani offer? His title *Homos* is designed to mark a distinction between his own work and queer theory by insisting upon the value of homosexuality – or what he calls 'homo-ness' – rather than simply seeking to dismantle the hetero/ homo binary and replace it with an unconstrained and largely free-floating model of desire. 'Homo-ness' directs attention to what is unassimilable in gay life, an embracing of sameness that challenges conventional ideas about community, yet which is also 'a mode of connectedness to the world that it would be absurd to reduce to sexual preference' (Bersani 1995: 10). In Bersani's view 'homo-ness' provides an indispensable opportunity for re-imagining both the self and the social by pushing them to their limits, by taking them beyond what we would ordinarily understand them to be.

In a way, Bersani's position could be described as simultaneously *pre-* and *post-*Foucauldian. His work is post-Foucauldian insofar as he accepts the claim made in *The History of Sexuality* that homosexuality was a product of late nineteenth-century medical and juridical thought, but believes that the lessons drawn from Foucault's genealogy have typically been too negative or too restrictive in their implications. It is 'almost as if homosexuality were nothing but a reaction, the responses of a social group to its own invention' (Bersani 1995: 33). Bersani therefore puts aside the project of historicizing homosexuality and turns for inspiration to three modernist writers who have pursued their own obsessive explorations of 'homo-ness' or 'desire for the same': André Gide, Marcel Proust and Jean Genet. In its attempt to find a more utopian space for gay desire, stepping outside the confines of contemporary theoretical debates, *Homos* is primarily pre-Foucauldian in its sources and in its substance, particularly where it draws upon (and invariably revises) psychoanalytic insights.

Bersani's readings are incisive and brilliantly creative, but they are not without their problems. Take, for example, Bersani's account of Gide's novel *L'Immoraliste* (1902), a book described by its author as a gorgeous 'fruit filled with bitter ashes', offering only a 'cruel fierceness' to the thirsty reader (Gide 1960: 7). In it Michel, a bookish young man who once cared for nothing but scholarship, tells how his discovery that he is suffering from tuberculosis while on honeymoon in Tunisia transformed him into an uncompromising hedonist. Bersani picks out two features of this narrative: the obscurity of Michel's transformation and the strangely contradictory nature of his pleasure-seeking. In Bersani's view it is not the threat of illness that changes Michel's life, but rather his 'discovery that he is a pederast' (Bersani 1995: 114). However, this apparently stark realization is not only something that Michel fails fully to understand, it is also complicated by his delight in other, less obviously sexual sensations. Which is perhaps why the closing lines of the novel strike such a curious note: Michel has returned to North Africa and begins to spend his nights with a beautiful young prostitute, but immediately gives her up when he finds out that his liaison is upsetting the woman's younger brother. In response she tells Michel that he 'prefer[s] the boy to her' and Michel tentatively admits that maybe 'she is not altogether wrong . . . ' (Gide 1960: 159).

What is odd here is Michel's belated, redundant admission of a preference that has been glaringly obvious all along and openly declared by Michel himself earlier in the book. How is it credible that Michel, in narrating his own transformation, did not know this? Bersani suggests that Michel's desire is less transparent than it seems, that his homosexuality is both 'unmistakable yet indefinable' (Bersani 1995: 116). And in truth Michel's epicurean sensuality really is peculiarly oblique, often solipsistic or remote. One of his most intense moments occurs on a visit to a lonely spot in Italy where, his body still exquisitely sensitive after the ravages of his illness, he takes off all his clothes and blissfully exposes himself to the sun. Bersani underlines the paradox at the heart of Michel's desires, variously referring to them as 'homosexuality without sexuality', a 'model for intimacies devoid of intimacy', invoking 'a community in which the other, no longer respected or violated as a person, would merely be cruised as another opportunity, at once insignificant and precious, for narcissistic pleasures' (Bersani 1995: 121, 128–9). In short, an 'anticommunitarian' community in which relationships are fleeting, elusive, attenuated to the point of absence.

The kind of self that such a 'chaste promiscuity' presupposes is mapped out during Michel's slow, solitary disrobing under the Italian sun (Bersani 1995: 125):

> The air was almost sharp, but the sun was burning. I exposed my whole body to its flame. I sat down, lay down, turned myself

about. I felt the ground hard beneath me; the waving grass brushed me. Though I was sheltered from the wind, I shivered and thrilled at every breath. Soon a delicious burning enveloped me; my whole being surged up into my skin.

(Gide 1960: 55)

For Bersani it is the concentration of feeling upon the surfaces of the skin that is so remarkable and so instructive in this passage. What has been lost is the capacity for immediate or instantaneous pleasure, suffocating under the deadweight of cultured learning. It is therefore necessary for Michel to give himself up 'to the luxurious enjoyment of my own self, of external things, of all existence, which seemed to me divine' (Gide 1960: 52). There are no hidden depths here, no long-buried interior self waiting to be revealed to the world. Instead, in Bersani's phrase, 'the authentic is the superficial' and Michel's being is absorbed into 'a desiring skin', a 'desire that is satisfied just by the proximity to the other, at the most by the other's touch (analogous to the touch of the soil and the grass on Michel's body)' (Bersani 1995: 120–1).

Born into a life of privilege Michel (*L'Immoraliste*) has set his face against the values of modern civilization that formerly provided the *raison d'être* of his scholarship. Even art comes to be seen as a life-denying force (since it opposes itself to the artistry of everyday living) while the stultifying necessity of manual work (together with marriage) is held responsible for destroying the beauty of young male bodies, as Michel discovers when he returns to the boys he left behind in North Africa. Bersani regards this as an invitation to imagine a new kind of erotic community freed from property relations in which bodies are, in the strictest sense, self-less: 'shifting points of rest in a universal and mobile communication of being' (Bersani 1995: 128). Yet to activate this interpretation Bersani has quickly to slide over the novel's sacrificial logic through which the price exacted for a fortified male homosexuality is an enfeebled and displaced femininity. Thus, just as the young Arab whore must be exiled from Michel's bed in order to release him into the company of boys, so his wife Marceline's tubercular lungs must fatally haemorrhage to enable Michel to 'feel the presence of happiness' in 'the midst of splendour and death' and to allow him 'to begin over again' (Gide 1960: 157–8). As Naomi Segal observes, this is precisely why 'Marceline must be brought to her final haemorrhage at the site of Michel's erstwhile rebirth' (Segal 1998: 187).

However, it is certainly possible to argue that these reservations do not altogether detract from *Homos*'s central point, namely that desire and pleasure are forces that have a devastating effect upon us and upon our ordinary social relationships. In fact, Bersani would probably want to claim that the perverse consequences of Michel's immoralism actually reinforce his thesis. Borrowing from the French psychoanalyst Jean Laplanche, Bersani refers to this experience of disruption as an effect of *ébranlement* (literally 'shock' or 'commotion') or what he calls 'self-shattering'. In self-shattering the subject's ego is thoroughly (if temporarily) undone and its boundaries begin to dissolve, loosening any clear sense of the difference between the self and others. Such ecstatic moments put at risk 'the whole concept of identity' and 'even more fundamentally, the notion of relationality itself' (Bersani 1995: 42, 52). Self-shattering offers us an intimation of what it might mean to speak of 'an anti-identitarian identity', an identity that would erase any trace of what identity once was (Bersani 1995: 101).

Obviously a lot is at stake here. Bersani claims, for example, that same-sex passion is transformed through self-shattering, since its 'privileging of sameness' now derives 'from the perspective of a self already identified as different from itself', that is from 'a desiring subject for whom the antagonism between the different and the same no longer exists' (Bersani 1995: 59–60). Sameness seems to have the capacity to absorb – or perhaps to neutralize – difference, disarming the threat of otherness. From this standpoint gender divisions appear to provide the occasion or the resources for their own supersession; for example, 'the gay man's deployment of signifiers of the feminine may be a powerful weapon in the defeat of those defensive maneuvers that have defined sexual difference'. Identifying with women or incorporating 'woman's otherness' into himself is part of a complex trajectory of desire in which nothing is fixed in advance:

> The gay man's identification with women is countered by an imitation of those desiring subjects with whom we have been officially identified: other men. In a sense, then, the very maintaining of the couples man-woman, heterosexual-homosexual, serves to break down their oppositional distinctions. These binary divisions help to create the diversified desiring field across which we can move, thus reducing sexual difference itself – at least as far as desire is concerned – to a merely formal arrangement inviting us to transgress the very identity assigned to us within the couple.
>
> (Bersani 1995: 61)

There are a number of points to make about this revealing passage. In the first place, one might question whether Bersani's psycho-analytically inspired description of the restless volatility of the desiring imagination cannot be applied to *all desire* and not just to that of the gay man. In the next chapter we shall see that some of the recent work on how readers and viewers involve themselves in literary and film texts suggests that Bersani's assumptions are less gay-specific than he tends to imply. For it may be that cross-identification provides the key to the intensest forms of visual and literary pleasure.

Indeed, the more Bersani stresses the mobility of subject positions and the instability and the inconvenience of desire, the more his argument begins to resemble the open-endedness of queer accounts of identity whose allegedly 'de-gaying' consequences he was at pains to critique. Part of his strategy for giving priority to sameness, while at the same time allowing free rein to difference, is to concentrate upon examples of gay texts that continue to confront the reader with their own provocative mode of *ébranlement*. But, as we saw in the case of Gide, attempts to move beyond gender divisions can sometimes merely strengthen them. For the violence and the pleasure of Michel's trangressions surely depend upon a series of gendered binaries through which the untamed Mediterranean landscape is conceived as an all-male preserve so hostile to feminine domesticity that a figure like Marceline cannot survive there. And, as Mandy Merck has observed in one of the most acute discussions of Bersani's work to date, to recognize this is to raise a far more difficult question for men and women, gay and straight alike: 'How might the gendered opposition of wild and tame, savagery and domesticity, be thought otherwise?' (Merck 1998: 235). That this question can even be asked may be one sign that Bersani's argument is far less radical than he would have us believe.

Yet, caveats aside, it is undeniably the case that in Bersani's work – as in the move from 'gay' to 'queer' more generally – we find the very notion of gendered identity placed under maximum pressure. Indeed, *Homos*, with its call for an experience of selfhood that is predicated upon its own dissolution, a mode of being that is at once ephemeral and episodic, a flux of pleasurable sensations and awesome intensities without an organizing centre, epitomizes the dilemmas faced by those who would seek an identity that does not simply mirror the alternatives offered by the straight world. Is such a search a contradiction in terms? Is the vocabulary in which we think about who we are so closely (and so damagingly) tied to the contrast between male and female subjects that, in order to do justice to the complexity of our desires, we need to abandon the lineaments of identity and begin to imagine a form of subjectivity that dispenses with the commonsense certainties of gender? For all its faults and incoherences, Bersani's polemic shows why such a post-identity theory might be indispensable and what it might look like. Too militantly suspicious fully to endorse the label of 'queer', he nevertheless allows his readers a taste of a queer future.

4

READERS AND SPECTATORS

Reading is now such a basic skill, seeming to transcend consider-
ations of gender, that it is hard to think of it as having a history at
all, let alone a past that belongs to the history of the relationship
between men and women. But the act of reading has itself varied
enormously over time, a fact that is immediately apparent from the
physical form that the written word has taken. If we think of the
elaborately illustrated manuscripts copied out by medieval scribes,
for instance, we are obviously in a different world from that
presupposed by the mass production of printed books. An early
fifteenth-century manuscript of Chaucer's *Troilus and Criseyde*
pictures the author reading his narrative poem to King Richard II
and Queen Anne surrounded by lords and ladies of the court, an
image that underscores the oral, performative character of reading
in an age of limited literacy. Indeed, in this period even reading to
oneself seems typically to have meant reading out loud. Thus, among
the rules of the early medieval Benedictine Order is a direction that
'[a]fter the sixth hour, having left the table let [the monks] rest on
their beds in perfect silence; or if anyone wishes to read by himself,
let him read so as not to disturb the others' (quoted in McLuhan

1969: 116). Reading might be an aid to meditation, but the fact that the words on the page are spoken could also undermine an atmosphere of concentration.

Here we have two brief examples of what might be called the *social relations of reading*. In the first, to put a text into circulation is to read it to an audience. Chaucer's purpose is informed by a deep moral seriousness: he wanted to contrast the love of Christ with the precariousness of worldly passion, setting the majesty of religion against the vicissitudes of courtly love, and the illustration shows him standing in an outdoor pulpit. Yet his poem was also written to entertain and to amuse, an emphasis that came to predominate in the more secular, post-medieval period. When printed books started to appear in court society they were

> intended less for reading in the study or in solitary leisure hours wrung from one's profession, than for social conviviality; they are a part and continuation of conversation and social games, or, like the majority of court memoirs, they are substitute conversations, dialogues in which for some reason or other the partner is lacking.

> (Elias 1982: 275)

Once again, reading has a public and occasional quality about it in that it is an extension of the everyday rituals and routines of courtly life. But Elias's description also hints at a more modern relationship to the book in which reading is a silent and deeply private experience, an inner colloquy that entails a withdrawal of the self from the social whirl. On this view the colourful portraits to be found in the seventeenth-century *Memoirs* of the Duc de Saint-Simon prefigure the minutely observed dissection of Parisian society two centuries later depicted in the novels of Balzac and Proust.

In general terms we can say that, despite its importance, the ability to read and write was an exceptional accomplishment until the middle of the sixteenth century. And only in the nineteenth century did literacy become at all commonplace. As David Cressy observes, 'England, for most of her history, has been a partially literate society, in which the art of writing and record-keeping was confined to a clerical, governmental and commercial elite' (Cressy 1990: 838). Reading, a skill that would have been learned before writing, was probably more widespread and was given a boost by the invention of printing, since standardized type was easier to read than handwritten script. Nevertheless, in the early years of printing the law was used to prevent some people from reading. An Act of 1543 outlawed the reading of the Bible in English among the ranks of the lower orders which included apprentices, yeomen *and* women.

It is hard to be sure how many people could read at any given time because, unlike writing, reading leaves no clear historical traces. A rise in the number of books or pamphlets undoubtedly shows an increase in the demand for reading material, but it is impossible to know exactly how many people could make use of it. However, taking the ability to sign one's own name as a rough guide to the distribution of literacy, it is clear that reading was a highly gendered activity. 'At the time of the English Civil War', says Cressy, 'more than two-thirds of all Englishmen – contemporaries of Milton and Cromwell – could not write their names', whereas for women the figure was 'as high as 90 per cent' (Cressy 1990: 844). This gap continued despite the fall in illiteracy rates, but with the growth of towns and cities as commercial centres we begin to see significant variations. In London, for example, about half the women had become literate by the 1690s, about the same proportion as for men in the English countryside, and this advance continued into the eighteenth century. It is against this metropolitan background that the plays, poems and novels by the female writer Aphra Behn (1640–89) need to be understood, with their trenchant critique of male power and gender ideologies.

If the cultural context of London life was crucial to Behn's achievement as one of the first women to make her living from writing, the absence of social support elsewhere created real obstacles. When

Anne Bradstreet's poem *The Tenth Muse Lately Sprung up in America* (1650) was first published in New England it was prefaced by a long apologia from her brother-in-law assuring readers that she had not neglected any of her womanly duties in making time to write. In colonial America many women seem to have been able to read, but they were not expected or encouraged to write. Michael Warner cites the example of a printer's wife in late seventeenth-century Maryland who set type and ran the press after her husband died, but could not sign her name. Until the end of the eighteenth century the schools that taught colonial American children to read were called 'woman schools', while those that taught them to write were known as 'masters' schools.' Women could not write without feeling some sense of inappropriateness or inhibition. 'To write', Warner emphasizes, 'was to inhabit gender' (Warner 1990: 15), but his aphorism is no less true of reading. Even instruction within the family was often gendered, the responsibility for teaching children to read being vested in the mother, while writing remained the pedagogic preserve of the father.

GENDER AND THE PUBLIC SPHERE

One of the most important developments arising from the spread of literacy in the late seventeenth century was the emergence of a new zone of free and open discussion, now known as the public sphere. Distinct from either the family or government or the royal court, this loose, unofficial network of social relations came into being through gatherings occurring in several different types of venue: receptions in salons or fashionable houses, meetings in private clubs and literary societies, casual conversations in coffee houses and taverns, all of them providing occasions when the leading issues of the day could be examined or thrashed out. What held these disparate encounters together (there were some 3,000 coffee houses in London alone in the early 1800s), informing and underpinning their many controversies and topical debates, was a rapidly expanding periodical press whose journals, featuring essays, criticism and poetry, were widely available in towns and cities. The public sphere was therefore more than simply a talking-shop; it was a highly literate urban reading public.

In his classic account of what he sees as the rise and subsequent decline of the public sphere, Jürgen Habermas (1962) claims that, at its best, it was distinguished by three mutually reinforcing characteristics. First, participants in the public sphere thought of it as an extended conversation among peers. Differences of social status were necessarily irrelevant to the clarity and cogency with which someone might convincingly state their case and thus should always be ignored. Moreover, in principle, discussion was open to anyone who had enough capital and education to enable them to become involved. And, by the same token, no one could ever be permanently disqualified from taking part. Finally and relatedly, debate was primarily conceived in terms of the exercise of one's reason, so that no subject was beyond rational criticism and all disputes could be settled through logical argument. Put like this, the public sphere appeals strongly to the most hopeful humanitarian values: the commitment to a judicious, dispassionate exchange of views between free and equal individuals.

Of course, the weaknesses inherent in this formulation are also obvious enough. In practice, as the historical data on illiteracy would lead us to expect, the eighteenth-century public sphere was confined to a relatively small minority of privileged people, typically men, for whom mercantile capitalism provided the money, leisure and expertise to take advantage of the opportunity to engage in 'rational-critical public debate' (Habermas 1989: 43). Habermas is, however, well aware of these objections, noting that in Britain, the earliest example of a flourishing public sphere, the mass of the population were 'so pauperized that they could not even pay for literature', whether they were able to read it or not (Habermas 1989: 38). So it is important to see exactly why Habermas regards the public sphere as such a major cultural advance.

What matters most to Habermas is that, through the public sphere, independent rational criticism became an ordinary everyday occurrence, producing a lively, knowledgeable citizenry, at least among members of the reformed aristocracy and the commercial middle classes who formed the readership of journals like *The Tatler*. The aim of popularizing ideas, of reaching the broadest possible 'publick', while raising the general standard of conduct and discussion, was enshrined in the pages of the periodical press, or what Habermas has dubbed 'the moral weeklies', from the outset. Writing in his paper *The Spectator* in March 1711, Joseph Addison declared that he would be pleased 'to have it said of me, that I have brought Philosophy out of Closets and Libraries, Schools and Colleges, to dwell in Clubs and Assemblies, at Tea-Tables and in Coffee-Houses' (Steele and Addison 1982: 210). His twelve essays on 'The Pleasures of the Imagination' which appeared in June and July the following year were precisely designed to instruct his readers in the subtleties of aesthetic discrimination, moving from the art of tea-drinking to the appreciation of fine writing and explicitly recommending 'Conversation with Men of a Polite Genius' as a 'Method for improving our Natural Taste' (366). Encouraged by such publications, men from different social classes turned their attention to literary and cultural questions, as well as to matters of politics and public affairs. They were able to pursue their arguments further through the letter columns of their favourite journals, a device that vastly extended the operations of the public sphere across time and space. At Button's Coffee House in London, for example, a lion's head was fixed to the wall 'through whose jaws the reader threw his letter' to *The Spectator* (Habermas 1989: 42). In such small details Habermas discerns the origins of modern democratic public opinion with its constitutionally guaranteed freedoms of speech, assembly and expression.

What of women readers? Habermas paints a complex picture. On the one hand, he recognizes that some key institutions like the coffee house were closed to women, despite their protests: hence the appearance of pamphlets like *The Women's Petition against Coffee, representing to Public Consideration of the Grand Inconveniences according to their Sex from the Excessive use of that Drying, Enfeebling Liquor* in 1674. On the other hand, he also suggests that 'the intimate sphere of the conjugal family created, so to speak, its own public', since the home was one of the private domains in which discussion could take place (29). At the grandest level, salons or receptions devoted to literature and the arts were largely organized and orchestrated by wealthy and influential women, especially in continental Europe, where they sometimes acquired a reputation as centres of political intrigue. In general, says Habermas, 'female readers as well as apprentices and servants often took a more active part in the literary public sphere' than male heads of households (56). Here, at least, women could distinguish themselves as something other than wives and mothers. Moreover, from the standpoint of 'the educated classes' the world of letters and that of political debate were two sides of the same coin: 'in the self-understanding of public opinion the public sphere appeared as one and indivisible' (56).

In their concern with manners and decorum, writers like Addison or Swift could be extremely condescending in their treatment of women. Addison's 1711 essay on 'the Faults and Imperfections of one Sex transplanted into another' is actually an occasion for mocking women's presumption in holding strong political views, chiefly on the grounds that they lack 'that Caution and Reservedness which are requisite in our Sex' and soon reveal their essentially emotional natures. Consequently,

> When this unnatural Zeal gets into them, it throws them into ten thousand Heats and Extravagances; their generous Souls set no Bounds to their Love, or to their Hatred; and whether a Whig or a Tory, a Lap-Dog or a Gallant, an Opera or a Puppet-Show, be the Object of it, the Passion, while it reigns, engrosses the whole Woman.
>
> (Steele and Addison 1982: 253)

Elsewhere, Addison distinguished between those women for whom 'the right adjusting of their Hair [forms] the Principal Employment of their Lives' and those 'reasonable Creatures' who 'move in an exalted Sphere of Knowledge and Virtue . . . and inspire a kind of Awe and Respect, as well as Love, into their Male-Beholders.' Part of his motive in writing is, he asserts, 'to encrease the Number' of the latter by diverting 'the Minds of my Female Readers from greater Trifles' (212). While couched in distinctly unflattering terms, Addison's tendentious contrast does have the effect of aligning a version of femininity with progress and civilization. As Jonathan Brody Kramnick has argued, it was 'the prominence of "gentle" readers from the "Female World," whose leisurely domesticity put "so much Time on their Hands" that augured the mannered elegance of modern English culture' which Addison and others sought to promote (Kramnick 1997: 1089).

However, the most comprehensive analysis to date of the female contribution to papers like *The Spectator* is far more pessimistic in its conclusions than Kramnick's brief but suggestive remarks on Addison and his circle might lead one to expect. In her 1989 study *Women and Print Culture*, Kathryn Shevelow surveys the overall pattern of development followed by the early periodicals and argues that, although the presence of women readers and writers indicates that they were able to make significant inroads into the male-dominated public sphere, the terms on which they entered tended to confirm their subordinate domestic status. To document her point, Shevelow compares John Dunton's *Athenian Mercury* from the 1690s with *The Tatler* and *The Spectator* nearly two decades later and notes their very different approaches to readers' letters. The *Mercury* was essentially an epistolary publication, consisting almost entirely of answers to queries raised by readers. For John Dunton women were a vital segment of his target audience and the first issue even carried a subtitle that promised to resolve 'all the most Nice and Curious Questions proposed by the Ingenious of Either Sex'. How many of the letters were genuine and how many were devised by journalists in pursuit of good copy it is impossible to say. But certainly the *Mercury* displayed advertisements encouraging correspondence from female readers on 'all manner of Questions' (Shevelow 1989: 60). Not so *The Tatler*. Despite the dubious 'Honour' of being 'invented' for 'the Fair Sex' (who 'tattle' or gossip), women were never meant to be the primary recipients of Richard Steele's periodical. Indeed, letters were not the mainstay of *The Tatler* at all, for it gave pride of place to essays or commentaries offered by a literary persona who would incorporate various communications, ranging from 'Letters of Gallantry' to letters from the country, into his ruminations or flights of fancy. Under Steele and Addison's editorship the periodical moved to a more tightly structured, rather 'monologic framework' in which 'the persona usurped the act of reader self-representation by determining its nature and its context'; hence the tendency for the 'I' of the essay to summarize or paraphrase or even ventriloquize his readers' observations, rather than allowing them the use of their own voices (106).

When Steele and Addison discuss the relations between men and women they are essentially writing as moralists. In his essay on 'Poor and publick whores' (1712), for example, Steele attacks for their lack of compassion those society ladies whom he dubs 'the outragiously virtuous', noting that although '[t]he unlawful Commerce of the Sexes is of all other [Sins] the hardest to avoid; . . . yet there is no one which you shall hear the rigider Part of Womankind speak of with so little Mercy' (Steele and Addison 1982: 266). As this comment suggests, for Steele and Addison morals and gender were inextricably linked. Thus in an earlier review in *The Tatler*, Steele had argued 'That the Soul of a Man and that of a Woman are made very unlike, according to the Employments for which they are designed', so that the 'Virtues have respectively a Masculine and a Feminine Cast'. Here the idealization of femininity is made possible through a parallel idealization of domesticity since, according to Steele, 'to manage well a great Family, is as worthy an Instance of Capacity, as to execute a great Employment' (156–7).

This doctrine of separate but complementary spheres – Steele is careful to say that men do not have 'superior Qualities' – also underwrites Addison's eulogy on the 'Pleasures' of 'a happy Marriage' with all its 'Enjoyments of Sense and Reason', from whose satisfied heights he deduced that 'Nothing is a greater Mark of a degenerate and vitious Age, than the common Ridicule which passes on this State of Life' (262). In the pages of *The Tatler* and *The Spectator* the elevation of women rested upon their effective confinement to the private domain of the home.

This raises a more general problem. As Shevelow points out, part of the market logic of including women in the periodical press was to move towards the specialization of content along gender lines. Publications that catered for women tended to concentrate upon 'Domestick Life' rather than 'Publick Affairs' and this was as true of the monthly 'ladies' issues' produced by the *Athenian Mercury* as it was of Eliza Haywood's *Female Spectator*, said to be the first periodical written by and for women and published nearly half a century later. To be sure, the latter represented an important new stage of development for, while it drew upon some of the essayistic conventions established by Steele and Addison, it also included readers' letters and fiction and, above all, relied explicitly upon the editorial identity of a female persona that 'substantially qualified or broke down altogether the hierarchical distance between writer and reader' typical of previous male-dominated publications (Shevelow 1989: 168). However, in adopting a more intimate form of address, the *Female Spectator* was continuing to reinforce the assumption that the social world could be divided between distinctively masculine and feminine modes of experience. This stance paved the way for the early women's magazines such as novelist Charlotte Lennox's *Lady's Museum* (1760) with its miscellany of poems, essays, serials, letters and illustrations; and by the mid-1770s titles like the *Matrimonial Magazine or Monthly Anecdotes of Love and Marriage* began to appear which also featured recipes, fashion items or needle-work patterns.

Shevelow believes that these publications not only 'offered images in which readers could locate themselves', but that they put in place an 'ideology of domesticity' whose final form was the claustrophobic patriarchal household typified by the Victorian phrase the 'angel in the house' (Shevelow 1989: 193). Read beside Shevelow's study, therefore, Habermas's claims regarding women's participation in the literary public sphere – at least if we take this as referring to those journals which tackle both political *and* cultural issues – start to look disappointingly thin. However, a thorough evaluation of the public sphere thesis also needs to consider Habermas's account of its decline as well as its rise, in other words its 'structural transformation'.

The test of whether this sphere of discussion and criticism could really be described as 'public' ultimately rested upon 'the principle of universal access'. Clearly, '[a] public sphere from which specific groups would be *eo ipso* excluded was less than merely incomplete; it was not a public sphere at all' (Habermas 1989: 85). Habermas's formulation suggests that the ideal was always flawed, or perhaps more accurately, that there was a gap between its universalistic pretensions and the narrow class and gender base of its main constituency. As Shevelow shows, while a journal like the *Athenian Mercury* was relatively even-handed in its treatment of middle-class male and female readers, women correspondents whose poor spelling and grammar and social circumstances placed them beyond the pale of bourgeois propriety were often denied a reply and could instead find themselves held up as a sad warning of 'what almost all those sort of *people* must at last come to' (Shevelow 1989: 213). The democratic struggles of the nineteenth century exacerbated these tensions and one effect of these new demands for political representation was a heightened sense of anxiety about readers and reading.

Victorian Britain can be described as a golden age of modern print culture. Between 1837 and 1901 something like 60,000 works of fiction were published, a figure that takes no account of the huge number of short stories in journals and magazines. And from the 1850s and 1860s we also see the growth of a new species of periodical, like the *Cornhill* or the *Saturday Review*, whose editors and authors were determined 'to establish between themselves and their readers common principles and standards on the major political, moral, religious, and cultural issues of the day' (Keating 1991: 35). Indeed, one could argue that this was a key phase in the development of what Habermas refers to as the literary public sphere.

Largely because of his predominantly eighteenth-century focus, Habermas tends to underestimate not only its complexity and importance, but also the central role played by women in the nineteenth-century world of letters. Throughout this period gender provided much of the vocabulary in terms of which judgements of literary success were made. So Charles Reade's highly praised, but now long-forgotten bestseller *It Is Never Too Late To Mend* (1856) was commended for the 'superb physical strength' of his writing, prose that was 'powerful', 'vigorous', 'lusty' and 'daring' and whose stirring narrative offered a welcome relief from 'the sentimental woes and drawingroom distresses which form the staple of so much of our circulating library fiction'. Nearly three decades later this sort of language was still in play in the obituary published by *Punch* magazine which contrasted Reade's 'virile creations' with the effete output characteristic of the many 'twaddlers tame and soft' whose work defaced the literary scene (Thompson 1996: 27–8). Signs of femininity were widely held to indicate a fatal weakness in a writer's style, so much so that Mrs Margaret Oliphant could applaud her fellow-author George Eliot for perfecting novels that were 'less definable in point of sex than the books of any other woman who has ever written' (Tuchman and Fortin 1989: 186). This kind of thinking, as Eliot herself keenly appreciated, placed women novelists in a double-bind. For if literary greatness was predicated upon their being able to negate or transcend their femininity, the critical esteem accorded to 'manly' writing seemed to condemn women to the perpetual risk of producing either pale imitations or hypermasculine caricatures.

Behind this dilemma lay the larger question of who controlled the literary public sphere. In their study *Edging Women Out*, Gaye Tuchman and Nina Fortin trace a growing male reaction against women's commercial success as novelists in the 1840s and 1850s and, using data from publishers' archives, they show how by the end of the nineteenth century more male authors were finding their way into print than their female counterparts, despite the fact that women submitted more manuscripts than men. Equally important, Tuchman and Fortin argue that by the 1870s male reviewers were beginning to employ gendered criteria to distinguish between serious fiction and popular entertainment. Male writing was said to display 'ideas capable of having an impact upon the mind', while women's novels were associated with ordinary feelings and the trivia of everyday life (78). But these and other, far harsher views had deep roots in the official culture of the Victorian era and could be found everywhere from medical texts to advice manuals. In E.J.Tilt's *On the Preservation of the Health of Women at the Critical Periods of Life* (1851), for example, there is a warning that:

> Novels and romances, speaking generally, should be spurned, as capable of calling forth emotions of the same morbid description which, when habitually indulged in, exert a disastrous influence on the nervous system, sufficient to explain that frequency of hysteria and nervous diseases which we find among the highest classes.
>
> (quoted in Flint 1993: 58)

Echoes of this same argument can still be heard at the century's close when Annie Swan, writing in answer to the question 'What Should Women Read?' in the periodical *Woman at Home*, insists that to dwell too much on women's 'imaginative and emotional side is to create the morbid' (61).

This is not the whole story. There is no shortage of essays proclaiming the necessity of 'food for the mind' or praising books as the medium of self-development *par excellence*. But the idea that a woman's reading capacities were always already inscribed in the female body itself, an integral part of her physiology, died hard and was reinforced by a tendency to associate other changes in the social order with feminine characteristics. As Andreas Huyssen has argued more generally, throughout late nineteenth-century Europe 'a specific traditional male image of woman served as a receptacle for all kinds of projections, displaced fears, and anxieties', so that a 'fear of the masses' was 'also a fear of woman, a fear of nature out of control, a fear of the unconscious, of sexuality, of the loss of identity and stable ego boundaries in the mass' (Huyssen 1986: 52). One can see this interpretive slide at work in the reception of the 'New Woman' fiction in Britain in the 1890s, texts in which their chiefly female authors attempted to challenge received ideas on sexuality, marriage, careers and health. Predictably, male critics were quick to diagnose this kind of writing as a 'literature of hysteria' or even 'a literature of vituperation and of sex-mania', a symptom 'of a restless and fretful age' likely 'to widen the breach between men and women, and to make them more mutually distrustful than ever' (Stutfield 1897: 109, 116). But, from a woman's perspective, what this often didactic fiction achieved was the opening up of a social space in which issues like venereal disease or the male double standard might be publicly discussed. In other words, the intimacy of the household could become a site of controversy, something like a feminized literary public sphere (see Flint 1993: 300). And it was these controversies that prepared the ground for women's suffrage.

However, there is an important qualification that needs to be entered here. The huge expansion in Victorian print culture meant that publishing of all kinds was gradually ceasing to be a 'small handicraft business' (Habermas 1989: 180). It now had the potential to become a large-scale commercial operation with a relatively small number of powerful, highly capitalized and technologically advanced companies reaching out to millions of readers. For Habermas, this move towards economic concentration combined with the growth of a mass audience spelled the end of the public sphere. In his view, by the close of the nineteenth century print was ceasing to provide a means by which men and women could engage in reasoned discussion of the major political issues that faced them, including, we might add, the question of their unequal relationship to each other, a point that Habermas has largely ignored. There is a very real paradox in Habermas's account of cultural change. For, as we saw earlier, the eighteenth-century public sphere may have facilitated remarkably open and democratic exchanges among the relatively small number of people who took part in it, but women were only allowed a subordinate role at best.

The creation of a truly mass audience initially took place in the newspaper industry where innovative printing techniques, new styles of popular journalism and a steady stream of advertising revenue helped to push daily circulation figures over the one million mark by the first decade of the twentieth century. If more men and women were reading newspapers than ever before, the industry's exceptional profitability meant that they were being served by extremely powerful financial interests. Whereas 'formerly the press was able to limit itself to the transmission and amplification of the rational-critical debate of private people assembled into a public', Habermas believes that the modern newspaper industry and the mass media more generally now tend to shape the terms in which the key national issues are posed from the outset. Another effect of this unprecedented growth has been to transform 'the public sphere into a medium of advertising' in which the reader is increasingly addressed as a consumer, rather than as a citizen (188–9). And insofar as the home has become the major site of consumption, women readers have become a new target audience, though whether this has resulted in their empowerment or simply in new ideologies of domesticity continues to remain a controversial topic. Certainly, these changes have raised ever more urgent questions about gender and the nature of reading under contemporary conditions, particularly given the tendency for texts to be organized into male and female genres. Can we still hold on to the notion of a literary public sphere once texts start to be marketed to a vast, anonymous and sometimes international pool of readers? Or, to paraphrase Terry Eagleton, has all discussion become absorbed into the culture industry (Eagleton 1984: 107)? Although writers like Habermas or Eagleton can make these sound deceptively like gender-neutral questions, they have frequently been framed and answered in gendered terms, whether wittingly or not.

'INTERPRETIVE COMMUNITIES'

As we saw in our brief account of the Victorian woman reader, the idea of a mass public has typically been a source of worry to the main centres of respectable middle-class opinion and has often been seen as possessing feminine characteristics. In the late 1850s the novelist Wilkie Collins was shocked to discover that 'the great bulk of the reading public of England' preferred 'penny-novel Journals' to his own novels, a semi-literate audience he half-imagined as 'two timid girls, who are respectively afraid of a French invasion and dragon-flies' (quoted in McAleer 1992: 1–2). But at least he believed that this 'unknown public' could be won over.

A long quotation from Collins's essay subsequently appeared as one of the epigraphs to Queenie Leavis's *Fiction and the Reading Public* (1932), one of the earliest attempts at a systematic analysis of the modern book market. But Leavis's forecast was far less optimistic than that of her predecessor. Surveying the use made of public libraries, for example, Leavis argued that, despite the achievement of universal literacy, 'the book-borrowing public has acquired the reading habit while somehow failing to exercise any critical intelligence about its reading' (Leavis 1979: 21). Among the factors she cited as responsible for this lack of discrimination was the role of women in selecting library books and thus determining what texts will enter the home. According to one librarian:

if a woman is taken up with a house all day, she doesn't want tales about married problems or misunderstood wives – she knows enough about these already; she can't be bothered with dialect after a day's work, and historical novels aren't alive enough. What she enjoys is something that is possible but outside her own experience. . . .

(Leavis 1979: 22–3)

For Leavis this turn to undemanding or escapist forms of literature represented the 'disintegration' of the serious reading public and in some respects her argument parallels the account of the structural transformation of the public sphere later advanced by Habermas. Both critics chart a process of decline from the eighteenth century to the present, much of it due to what Leavis calls 'the increasing control by Big Business', though she also mentions other causes like the growing anti-intellectualism of a governing class whose men are expected to be 'simple but virile' rather than cultured and intelligent (29, 155). Leavis's account of the degradation of reading therefore seems to involve the feminization of a culture that upper-class men had largely abandoned. However, while she fails to think through the gender implications of this line of analysis, Leavis does paint a picture of a society in the grip of a shallow, feminine emotionalism. To help flesh out this claim she uses the impressionable figure of Gerty MacDowell from Joyce's *Ulysses* to epitomize the modern reader, characterizing her as a young woman whose predigested attitudes are drawn from 'memories of slightly similar situations in cheap fiction', who 'thinks in terms of clichés drawn from the same source, and is completely out of touch with reality'. The imaginary Gerty is thus all too 'typical of the level at which the emotional life of the generality is now conducted' (195–6).

In attempting to explain the success of the popular fiction of her day, Leavis argues, largely on the basis of extracts from readers' letters supplied by twenty-five authors, that these kinds of novels 'excite in the ordinary person an emotional activity for which there is no scope' in modern life. But precisely why emotional expression is assumed to be blocked among the majority of the population remains unclear. Leavis variously points to the decline of religion, to the failure of many modern individuals to develop fully, and to the effects of an increasingly specialized division of labour. Yet, while she does concede that novelists like Marie Corelli or Florence Barclay are 'genuinely preoccupied with ethical problems', her steadfast belief that these texts have very little redeeming value prevented her from looking closely at how they were read and how the act of reading was related to the reader's social situation (63).

The sorts of assumption informing Leavis's study were fairly commonplace among cultural critics in the 1930s and it took several decades before they came under scrutiny, not to say empirical investigation. To gauge the extent to which the questions asked about readers have changed in recent years, the best place to start is Janice Radway's *Reading the Romance* (1984), first published a little over half a century after Leavis's book first appeared. In broad outline *Reading the Romance* is not hard to summarize, though its detailed findings are sometimes quite complex. What Radway does is to take one of the most despised categories of popular writing discussed in *Fiction and the Reading Public* (though neither Leavis nor her book are explicitly mentioned by name) and try to show that there is more to domestic romance or the romantic novel than critical prejudice would lead one to expect. Her boldest move is to shift the spotlight away from the formal properties of literary narratives and on to the meanings that women readers 'find' there. This might sound as if reading is a purely individual or subjective affair, a matter of each reader's uniquely personal relationship to a given text. But, following the work of theorist Stanley Fish, Radway regards reading as an act that occurs within a *community* of readers using the same 'interpretive strategies': in other words, what a text is and how it might be read are to be understood through the shared conventions and social values of an 'interpretive community' (Fish 1980: 161).

The setting for Radway's research is the suburb of a midwestern American city she calls by the pseudonym Smithton, a site partly chosen because of its physical and cultural distance from New York where most of the publishing industry's major decisions are made. Radway focuses upon a network of women grouped around a bookseller named Dorothy Evans who published a regular newsletter that served as a guide to her customers and fellow readers by reviewing new titles, offering information and, perhaps most important of all, defending romance fiction against the ridicule that has often been heaped upon it in the press, the home and the workplace. This advisory and ideological work required a delicate sense of balance, moving between the authors and New York editors who increasingly sought her advice on their manuscripts and the regular romance readers who turned to her to help them save time and money. Dot's proudest boast was that she would never usurp her customers' 'right to choose their own reading materials', limiting herself only to making suggestions 'from my own experience'. So while her judgements necessarily reinforced well-worn genre categories, she was also careful to insist on 'respecting [the] personal preferences' of her readers (Radway 1987: 52–3).

As well as looking at Dot's pivotal opinion-shaping role, Radway carried out in-depth studies of forty-two of her female newsletter subscribers, asking them questions about their lives and their tastes in fiction. Her findings defy neat enumeration, for romance reading is revealed as an 'indistinct' or multifaceted activity, a 'complicated, polysemic event' (209). It is not possible to infer unambiguously from their reading whether these romance novels either help to reconcile these women to their lives or make them more restless, more critical. Not all romances are equally successful, for example, and those that are judged to fail do so because, however absorbing they might be, ultimately they leave their readers without a sense 'that men and marriage really do mean good things for women' (what Radway calls 'the promise of patriarchy') and consequently impair their feelings of self-worth and self-confidence (184). On the other hand, the social meaning of romance does not reside solely between its covers. Radway suggests that the act of reading itself, regardless of a particular novel's content, is simultaneously 'combative and compensatory' for these women:

> It is combative in the sense that it enables them to refuse the other-directed social role prescribed for them by their position within the institution of marriage. In picking up a book, as they have so eloquently told us, they refuse temporarily their family's otherwise constant demand that they attend to the wants of others even as they act deliberately to do something for their own private pleasure. Their activity is compensatory, then, in that it permits them to focus on themselves and to carve out a solitary space within an arena . . . where they are defined as a public resource to be mined at will by the family.
>
> (Radway 1987: 211)

What matters most of all, therefore, is that reading the romance signifies a break in family time, a point of relief or suspension within the everyday that arises out of, but is countermanded by, ordinary domestic routine. The keen sense of disappointment that is sometimes aroused by an unsatisfactory text is a product not just of the puncturing of utopian desire, but derives from the highly charged, intensely cathected moment in which reading takes place. Because the reader is literally pleasing herself, the temporary deferral of her responsibilities to others creates a volatile mixture of hope and a sense of guilt that can easily be triggered by frustrated narrative expectations.

Radway's account of why these women read romances could be said to follow a kind of situational logic that is based upon the fit between the properties of the genre and the lives led by her respondents. Yet what bonds the women to their preferred texts is not their experience alone, but their involvement and participation in a collective discourse about romance reading that articulates their opinions and their enthusiasms. This discursive field or tradition serves as the medium through which the act of reading takes place, infusing it with meaning and value, principally via the circulation of Dot's newsletter. 'Dorothy's Diary of Romance Reading' activates the Smithton women's 'interpretive community', making texts and readers what they are.

It is important not to literalize the notion of 'community' in this formulation. The Smithton women are not readers who are organized or who meet regularly. Rather, they represent a virtual community or a symbolic community, linked solely by the values which they share. As Radway notes:

> Because the oppositional act is carried out through the auspices of a book and thus involves the fundamentally private, isolated experience of reading, these women never get together to share either the experience of imaginative opposition, or, perhaps more important, the discontent that gave rise to their need for the romance in the first place. The women join forces only . . . in the privacy of their own homes and in the culturally devalued sphere of leisure activity.

> (Radway 1987: 212)

Radway is therefore in no doubt that ultimately romance reading 'leaves unchallenged the male right to the public spheres of work, politics, and power' (217). In short, despite the self-awareness that the newsletter provides, this fragmented reading public lacks the cultural resources to challenge the terms of its own fragmentation.

Although she emphasizes the role played by a communal discourse in sustaining their reading habits, Radway often writes as if there were a natural affinity between women readers and romance novels. Indeed, if one reads Radway's study in tandem with, say, Ken Worpole's essay 'The American Connection: Masculine Style in Popular Fiction' (1983), it is easy to build up a somewhat exaggerated picture of how reading is gendered. Worpole argues that from the mid-1930s onwards many British working-class male readers found in American writers a tough vernacular realism that seemed to resonate with their own experiences of the harsh realities of living and working in the city. Yet Worpole is particularly concerned with those men who were politically active and his anecdotal evidence seems to suggest that it was their socialist ideology that drew them to the critique of urban corruption in novelists like Upton Sinclair and also in the hard-boiled detective fiction of Dashiell Hammett. Put another way, it is likely that socialist ideas provided the leading element in the popular aesthetic (or 'interpretive strategies') that governed or structured these men's mode of reading. By contrast, the Smithton women's preferences appear far more indeterminate. For, in their case, the suspension of time inherent in the act of reading is potentially compatible with a whole variety of genres or sub-genres (the racing thrillers written by Dick Francis have a wide female readership, for example). Yet, in practice, they seem to ignore these alternatives. One weakness of *Reading the Romance* is that, for all its plausibility, it does not entirely explain why it is this particular literary formula that appeals to the women Radway studied rather than another.

On the other hand, there are some indications that Radway's sample is unusual. They are remarkably dedicated readers and very few are 'avid television watchers'; rather surprisingly over half the sample never watched soap operas (Radway 1983: 76). As Steven Connor has warned, there is a danger here of 'turning commercial into ethnographic homogeneity' and then of mistakenly assuming that this group is 'typical of the readers of mass-market fiction'. Before jumping to conclusions we should consider the possibility that:

> Romances are not read only by romance readers but also by readers who are not 'romance readers' (academics, for example), or who will not remain so, or who have not always been so, or who are only occasionally so (though they may be intensely loyal during the periods when they are); to specify only these variables.
>
> (Connor 1996: 21)

Connor's point is that reading is generally far more fluid (or mutable) than Radway can envisage, especially under (post)modern conditions. Today, readers are increasingly likely to have what Connor calls 'multiple allegiances', moving between different kinds of fiction and different kinds of reading experience. This may well be true, but we can also turn this argument around by suggesting that the act of reading is *in itself* characterized by a greater degree of *interior* (or psychic) mobility than *Reading the Romance* is prepared to allow. Much of the psychoanalytically inspired work on fantasy and fantasy scenarios stresses that the process of identification is not fixed but passes from character to character, so that crossing the boundaries of gender can be an integral part of the reader's imaginative absorption in narrative time (see Kaplan 1986). Responding to this criticism, Radway has conceded the possibility that women 'readers do not identify only with the romantic heroine but in fact identify in multiple and wandering fashion with the seducer, the seduced and the process of seduction itself' (Radway 1987: 243). And elsewhere, pushing this point one step further, she has begun to see modern subjectivity as 'nomadic', shifting 'actively, discontinuously . . . via disparate associations and relations through day-to-day existence' (Radway 1988: 366). The wheel has come full circle.

But in neither Radway's early nor her slightly later arguments does reading figure as anything other than an individual practice. So, instead of swinging quickly from one style of analysis to its polar opposite, it is worth pausing for a moment to consider some of the evidence about the *social* occasions of reading, limited though this is. In fact, organized reading groups have a long and by no means negligible history, one that often connects them to the ideal of a public sphere. At the turn of the nineteenth century, American reading circles were linked to the women's club movement, for example, and in Texas in the Progressive Era women's reform groups also grew out of literary societies or book discussion groups. Indeed, according to current British research, reading groups continue to have 'a discernible civic dimension' in which serious reading is conceived as a means towards becoming a responsible and 'fully informed' member of society (Hartley 1999: 18). Political activity can bring reading circles into existence too, though sometimes indirectly: one of the Texas groups studied by Elizabeth Long (1986) in the early 1980s had its origins a quarter of a century earlier in a network of League of Women Voters members.

The women in the four groups in Long's exploratory study were therefore very different from those in Radway's sample. They were typically college-educated, belonged to affluent, white middle-class families, and tended to be in full-time professional jobs. The groups ranged in size from seven to nineteen members and would read a mixture of novels and nonfiction, excluding only those texts that they considered downmarket, undemanding or 'trashy' (reading romances or thrillers was out of the question, though an exception might be made for a writer like Dorothy L. Sayers). Books were selected according to an implicit 'hierarchy of taste' based upon 'a vague humanism that defines reading truly great books as a morally and intellectually enhancing experience' or, in the case of nonfiction, because of their 'social relevance' (Long 1986: 598–9). While such judgements display a marked deference to established centres of cultural authority such as universities or élite cultural journalism, they are not set in stone: the *New York Times Book Review* started to fall out of favour once it began including genre fiction and mass-market paperbacks.

However, once a book has been chosen, its treatment in the reading groups is not particularly reverent or constrained. The women describe their discussions as 'playful', by which they mean that their talk is allowed to jump from topic to topic, and also that they 'are willing to entertain a variety of readings' (603). What matters in discussions is not so much the free expression of opinion as the tacit granting of permission 'to take risks by making idiosyncratic connections, to bring forward personal experiences, to play with categories': there is little evidence of any 'interpretive community' at work during group meetings (604). Within the general rubric of seriousness that legitimates the group, reading can combine a sense of exhilaration with self-exploration or self-analysis. Although its somewhat anarchic clamour of different points of view reflects the individualistic values of modern American life, the pleasure taken in the free play of ideas means that, unusually, these discussions are regarded as valuable in themselves rather than simply being a means to an end.

But is there anything distinctively feminine about such groups? This is a very difficult question to answer. Long's subsequent work suggests that women are far more likely than men to start or join a reading circle. Out of over seventy reading groups she located in Houston, Texas, forty-two were women's groups, twenty-eight were mixed, but only three consisted solely of men. Long provides little systematic information about the latter, but at least some of her evidence from the mixed groups shows male readers gaining insight into their childhood through memories released by reading about fictional characters in a way that is similar to the responses of women readers. However, these reactions are not necessarily typical of male readers and may possibly be encouraged by the experience of reading with women. For, as Long stresses, 'women seem especially to merge psychological boundaries in this fashion' (Long 1987: 320). Nevertheless, it is clear that the male *and* female readers whom she studied shared a broad commitment to an unexamined realist aesthetic in which the credibility and psychological interest of the narrative reside in the possibility of identifying with its principal characters. And in this they seem to differ from the women whose reading consists exclusively of fiction such as romance aimed specifically at a female audience, since Radway's respondents and also most of the women who took part in Bridget Fowler's recent survey of Scottish romance readers, actively distinguish their preferred genre from the realist novel. In the eyes of these readers 'formulaic romance' provides 'an idealised vision of an unalienated, yet hierarchical society' in which 'patriarchy fosters protective love and true nobility of mind justifies privilege'. For those who are 'enmeshed within the confines of kinship and still dependent economically on men' it remains 'the "dream-book" of the family' (Fowler 1991: 175).

SPECTATEUR, SPECTATRICE

If late twentieth-century publishing increasingly became a department or specialism within vast multi-media conglomerates, it is also the case that for many men and women reading novels is now inseparable from their wider consumption of cultural narratives via film and television. To a large extent, these media currently occupy the space that once belonged to the literary public sphere and they are among the primary sites within which our sense of ourselves as gendered subjects or individuals is imaginatively engaged and tested out across a variety of cultural forms. The multiplier effect of one cultural form upon another can be considerable. To take a relatively small example: the release of the Merchant-Ivory film of E.M. Forster's *A Room with a View* in 1985 led to the sale of two million copies of the novel, compared to a mere 50,000 in Forster's own lifetime (Glover 1996: 30). As we have already noted, in Habermas's view this massification of the media and their concentration in the hands of a small number of giant corporations have been central to the public sphere's decline, turning a 'culture-debating' public into an audience of culture-consumers (Habermas 1989: 159). In the remainder of this chapter we will look at some of the weaknesses of Habermas's position from a gender perspective.

While Habermas has recently conceded that his original analysis was 'too pessimistic', partly because it ignored 'the cultural context of [media] reception', his model of the public sphere was also flawed by his idealization of print culture and his corresponding failure to address fully its tendency to exclude female participants (Habermas 1992: 427–8, 438–9). At one level these criticisms suggest some fairly straightforward revisions. By simultaneously questioning the assumptions behind Habermas's model and taking a fresh look at the history of the cinema, for example, it should become possible to bring women back into the picture. However, as we will see, it is debatable whether Habermas's thesis can really survive this kind of close, gender-sensitive scrutiny.

To begin at the beginning: one of the main themes in debates about the impact of film on early twentieth-century society was a fear that it would radically destabilize the relations between the sexes. 'Worst of all,' opined the *Chicago Daily News* in 1907, the new cheap movie theatres or nickelodeons 'may become foci for the spread of moral degradation', places where 'young girls particularly are in danger of forming associations that are ruinous' (quoted in Rabinovitz 1990: 74). Behind the paper's vague, yet undeniably sensationalizing language lay a number of what it believed were worrying developments: the rapid migration into Chicago of people new to American city life, especially young (often immigrant) working-class women, who were able to evade the control of their families in the vast metropolis. Again and again, gullible young women cinema-goers were identified as *the* problem generated by the new medium. In his satirical essay 'The Little Shopgirls Go to the Movies', written in Germany in the 1920s, cultural critic Siegfried Kracauer turned this prejudice on its head and cynically suggested a two-way relay between cinema and society: if 'sensational film hits and life usually correspond to each other' it is 'because the Little Miss Typists [*Tippmamsells*] model themselves after the examples they see on the screen', but it may also be 'that the most hypocritical instances are stolen from life' (Kracauer 1995: 292). In film it was possible to have the worst of both worlds.

This mixture of condescension and alarm was not untypical. On the one hand, women were attacked for failing to conform; on the other, they were ridiculed if they were seen as conforming too much. Cinema appears therefore as a potential site of transgression, a setting that allows women to reveal their troubling otherness, their appetites and their desires. Above all it provided access to new experiences. In

1897 one of the most popular attractions in American movie theatres was a film of a heavyweight boxing championship that ran for nearly two hours. What was truly remarkable was that 60 per cent of the audience consisted of women who, through the medium of film, were for the first time able to watch an intensely physical contest usually reserved for the gaze of men only. Under these novel relations of spectatorship boxing became visible as a sexually charged event.

Miriam Hansen, who opens her book *Babel and Babylon: Spectatorship in American Silent Film* (1991) with this vignette, has argued that the vogue for *The Corbett-Fitzsimmons Fight* among women breached 'the taboo on an active female gaze', reversing the widespread assumption that it was men who alone possessed the right to look. She reads this episode as a symptom and sign of the emergence of what she regards as 'an alternative public sphere' for women, a space within which their needs and aspirations could be articulated, in however tentative a form. Drawing upon Oskar Negt and Alexander Kluge's critique of Habermas in *Öffentlichkeit und Erfahrung* (1972; translated as *The Public Sphere and Experience*, 1993), Hansen's methodology locates this female counter-public negatively, searching for those practices that seem to stand out *against* the dominant order of the modern city and were subject to regulation or adverse comment. Unlike Habermas's concept of a public sphere, this alternative domain is disorganized, fleeting, evanescent: it springs to life in brief flashpoints or partial traces. Since female suffrage was not achieved until after the First World War, the women who frequented the movies during this period had little opportunity to participate in organized politics; indeed, a remarkably detailed unpublished study of German women spectators by Emilie Altenloh in 1914 actually observed that '[w]hile the men are attending political meetings, women visit the movie theater next door where they'll be met by their spouses when the screening is over' (quoted in Hansen 1983: 178). At the same time, the cinema was one of the few forms of leisure available to working-class women outside the home that was not an exclusively male preserve. It was cheap and also convenient enough to be squeezed into the interstices of an ordinary day, as part of a shopping trip or on the way home from work, and this mundane accessibility appealed to more affluent women too. Not only was a cross-class audience coming into existence, but there is evidence of some convergence between the classes; Altenloh noted 'a remarkably homogeneous attitude toward the cinema' among her female respondents, despite differences of class and marital status (Petro 1989: 19). In a sense, the early silent cinema capitalized upon and extended the reach of the new consumerist economy, epitomized by the department store and the advertisement hoarding, in which women made the main purchasing decisions for the household.

No matter how much or how little money these women had, cinema offered them 'a spectacle to be consumed' (Mayne 1988: 78). Because of the growing prominence of female spectators within the movie audience, films began to appear which directly addressed them in a variety of forms. Serials like *The Hazards of Helen* (1914) 'featured adventurous, physically active heroines' and provided 'pleasure in images of female competence, courage, and physical movement' (Hansen 1991: 120). Although there were more demure images of femininity in the persons of Lilian Gish or Mary Pickford, representing the conventionally compliant face of domestic virtue, the figure of the spirited modern girl continued into the 1920s through such actresses as Gloria Swanson. But, for Hansen, the star who most dramatically threw the contradictions of female spectatorship into relief was the matinée idol Rudolph Valentino. In the course of an unusually short film career – he first began to attract attention in 1917, yet by 1926 he was dead – Valentino not only made women swoon, his appearances could lead to minor riots.

Valentino's devoted following shows how the emerging star system was able to give expression to modes of female desire that were deeply at odds with the patriarchal cast of American culture. In the first place, Valentino's star persona combined considerable exotic allure with a curiously indeterminate eroticism. As a wild Arab chief, a French nobleman or as a Latin-American horseman and dancer, Valentino was both a sexual predator and a more ambiguous figure whose dress and demeanour often seemed to feminize him. Moreover, the very fact that the films frequently made him the recipient of a prolonged female gaze, an object of spectacular sensuality, served to invert the usual 'gender economy of vision' in which it is the woman whose desirability interrupts the forward movement of the narrative. But if Valentino appears to occupy the filmic position traditionally reserved for the woman, it is also crucial that his own gaze will eventually be brought into play, that *he* is shown to be a desiring subject who can bestow the gift of sexual rapture. However, neither of these moments is ever fully resolved: Hansen insists that Valentino's look and the identification it provokes are always characterized by an ineradicable ambivalence. Even when the actor's eyes are 'riveted on the woman of his choice, he seems to become paralyzed rather than aggressive or menacing' (279). In the Valentino text, mastery is always ready to yield to vulnerability.

Second, Valentino's extraordinary appeal to female viewers was extended and consolidated through the medium of publicity: fan clubs and magazines, interviews, competitions and special events. This was a mixed blessing for the movie industry. For although the function of the star system was to guarantee and then intensify the spectator's psychic and emotional attachment to each individual film, the creation of the star's persona, of an imaginary identity believed to exist outside the frame of the cinematic text, could also operate in the opposite direction so that visual pleasure was no longer concentrated in the narrative but was instead dissolved into 'a string of spectacular moments that display the "essence" of the star' (247). In such a system the careful management of the fans themselves is inevitably a sensitive issue, since they form a collective body whose legitimacy derives from their claim to have brought the star into existence by their own grassroots support; and the fan subculture invariably has the potential to get out of control. In the case of

Valentino the relationship between star and female fans was peculiarly obsessive and fetishistic and soon outstripped the bounds of moral and sexual propriety. When women sent him their 'intimate garments' in the mail requesting that he kiss and return them, he apparently did so (294). As part of his erotic 'pact' with his fans, Valentino arranged to have his corpse displayed before them after his death, to tumultuous effect. It is therefore possible to read the scenes of mass hysteria occasioned by his funeral not just as a collective expression of grief at the loss of an icon, but as a kind of last-ditch revolt by Valentino's fans against the demise of a symbolic world in which the narrow confines of gender no longer obtained.

This vision of an alternative public sphere is a far cry from anything in Habermas. Yet it should be remembered that Hansen is not concerned with the possibilities for rational-critical debate, but with the opening up of what Negt and Kluge term a new 'social horizon of experience', a place where 'needs, conflicts, anxieties, memories, and fantasies' can begin to achieve 'public recognition' (92). Her arguments are cautious, necessarily provisional and carefully qualified: since it is hard to know how these women 'received the films they saw and what significance moviegoing had in relation to their lives', the best that we can do is to 'try to reconstruct the configurations of experience that shaped their horizon of reception, and ask how the cinema, as a social and aesthetic experience, might have interacted with that horizon' (101). In a nutshell, Hansen's credo presents the abiding methodological dilemma confronting all historically based reception studies where first-hand accounts are unavailable, as they almost invariably are.

The most common route out of this impasse is to sift through the film review pages of newspapers and magazines in search of clues to the discursive or ideological context within which viewing took place. This is the approach adopted by Janet Staiger in her book *Interpreting Films* (1992), an avowedly Marxist analysis of the history of reception in American cinema, one of whose main tasks is to distinguish between the use of 'dominant' and 'marginal' interpretive strategies among film spectators at any given cultural and political moment. Staiger's work is often ingenious: when considering the reception of the Judy Garland movie *A Star is Born* (1954), for example, she takes the opinions voiced by reviewers in the mainstream press as the dominant or hegemonic responses to the film and then takes these as the benchmark against which 'alternative readings' can be defined as the ones 'that do not match' (Staiger 1992: 157). She is especially interested in explaining the Judy Garland cult among gay men, but her immediate practical difficulty is that the criminal status of homosexuality in the 1950s effectively outlawed any written record of how the film and its star were regarded at the time of its release. Staiger solves this problem by taking the later writings of gay critics like Jack Babuscio and Richard Dyer and then reading them back into the earlier context in order to show how they focus on aspects of *A Star is Born* that were overlooked by mainstream reviewers. Her warrant for this interpretive move is the development of a new gay cultural criticism as part of the struggle for gay rights following the 1969 Stonewall riots in New York, events that coincided with Garland's death in June of that year. However, Staiger has to assume that this watershed in gay politics created the conditions in which long-suppressed ideas could be made public, a conjecture that begs the question of whether Dyer or Babuscio's readings really can provide an accurate guide to how gay spectators saw the film several decades ago. In the absence of any reliable evidence Staiger can only hope that oral history will bridge the gap at some point in the future.

In their different ways both Staiger and Hansen set their face against the kind of analysis that regards the spectator's response as always already encoded into the filmic text. Some of the most widely discussed work on cinema proceeds on this basis. So, for example, Laura Mulvey's seminal essay 'Visual Pleasure and Narrative Cinema' draws upon psychoanalysis in order to argue that looking is typically divided 'between active/male and passive/female' components. That is to say, in terms of the positions offered to the spectator in mainstream cinema, the 'determining male gaze projects its fantasy on to the female figure', while 'women are simultaneously looked at and displayed' and are the object of 'erotic contemplation' (Mulvey 1989 [1975]: 19). And in a similar vein, Steve Neale has suggested that the male body cannot comfortably be subjected to the same voyeuristic scrutiny as the woman's for fear of the homosexual undertones this may evoke. Consequently the spectator's absorption in the fight scenes of a western or a thriller has a protective quality, denying any hint of an erotic subtext: masculinity is to be tested or proved rather than looked at (Neale 1983).

By contrast, Staiger seeks to account for reader response without privileging a psychoanalytic reading of the cinematic text. For her, psychoanalysis is merely one interpretive strategy among others and what matters is the extent of its influence in any particular historical period. In Staiger's view there can be no text without an audience for, without people to interpret it, it could have no meaning: a proposition that she shares with Stanley Fish, though she deploys it to somewhat different ends. As we have seen, Hansen's *Babel and Babylon* also aims to contextualize the act of viewing but, rather than dispensing with the filmic text, her approach is to historicize the text-centred model of gendered spectatorship advanced by Mulvey and others by claiming that what it really describes are the standardized 'modes of organizing vision and structuring narratives' put in place by classic Hollywood cinema from roughly the 1920s to the 1970s (Hansen 1991: 249). The value of studying early silent film is therefore that it allows us to see a looser, less monolithic set of relations between films and their spectators in operation *before* the Hollywood mass audience had been fully formed. And it allows us 'to take the spectator seriously as a productive force' that can never be wholly swallowed up by the movie industry (89).

Today the spectator is arguably less in thrall to Hollywood cinema than ever before. For despite the importance of feature films to the television industry, the rise of video, satellite and cable has altered the relationship between the public and the private once again.

Whereas cinema broke with the private conditions of reading by setting narrative and fantasy in public space, now 'the compulsive temporality of public projection has given way to ostensibly more self-regulated yet privatized, distracted and fragmented acts of consumption', placing new stresses upon men and women in the home (Hansen 1993: 198). This is not to say that privatized viewing is completely replacing collective forms of spectatorship. The weekly American ritual of watching *Dynasty* in gay bars discussed by Jane Feuer in her study of 1980s' television is an important contemporary example of the 'subcultural appropriation of a text', a moment of collective identity in a political climate not noticeably hospitable to gay rights (Feuer 1995: 135). And the development of the kind of intensive fan culture vividly portrayed in Constance Penley's work on 'slash fandom' points to some dramatic new possibilities for, not only interpreting, but completely reconfiguring popular narratives (see ch.2).

The Kirk/Spock fanzines and re-edited videos go beyond the imitative idolization of stars – singing their songs, acting out scenes from their films – traditionally associated with their followers (see Stacey 1994). Penley argues that in re-imagining the working partnership between the captain and first officer in terms of a 'passionate lifetime union' these fanzines not only rewrite the codes of the romance genre, but also construct 'new versions of female pornography' through the invention of a guardedly non-heterosexual form of masculinity (Penley 1992: 490–1). These subcultures are part of a wider phenomenon of 'textual poaching' which overturns many of the assumptions upon which spectatorship is often thought to be based, giving it a more intensively performative twist. The world of the fan is:

> characterized precisely by its refusal to respect cultural hierarchies (the boundary between high and low culture); its rejection of aesthetic distance (the boundary between text and reader); its blurring of distinctions between individual texts, genres, even

media; its defiance of conventional conceptions of literary property (the boundary between reader and writer); and its attempt to integrate media content into its everyday social experiences (the boundary between fantasy and reality).

(Jenkins 1990: 151)

But, as we have seen, the irreverence of the fanzine world is far from innocent of gender politics. Cheek by jowl with K/S romances we find songs like Dennis Drew's version of 'I Need A Little Girl' which paradoxically uses the image of an alien woman with dorsal fins and an extra eye to reinstate the normality of male heterosexual desire, a desire that is given a humorous if disturbing inflection, yet which is also reassuringly the same as it has always supposedly been (Jenkins 1990: 161–2).

The highly engaged modes of viewing discussed by critics like Constance Penley and Henry Jenkins belong to the new technological world of electronic reproduction and look forward to the consolidation of new types of fan culture via the worldwide web or the internet. Whether the enhanced possibilities for manipulating the image will completely change the conditions of spectatorship remains to be seen; though it is worth noting that among the fans studied by Penley the distinction between reader, viewer and writer is constantly blurred. If these viewers of *Star Trek* belong to one of the most creative audiences that have ever appeared, promoting extrordinarily sophisticated fantasies and identifications – Kirk and Spock are felt to have revealed themselves as more desirable because their romantic natures have been demonstrated on screen through a relationship between them that curiously *cannot* be imagined as gay – it is nevertheless also true that these female fans see their interpretations 'as amplifying rather than negating or deforming the text', bringing out elements that were already implicit within it (Penley 1989: 259). Though their adaptations have scandalized the ordinary *Star Trek* enthusiasts, trespassing upon the sacred preserve of the text, K/S fans regard their activities in a properly conservative light, 'reading with the grain' of the narrative instead of brushing against it. Here, at the crossroads of the future, cross-identifications are more star-crossed than ever as the lines between genders become hopelessly entangled in the wake of authentic desire.

The K/S appropriation of *Star Trek* returns us to many of the issues considered in this chapter and elsewhere in this book. For the practices of these fans enact a virtual stand-off between corporate capitalism, as represented by the owners of *Star Trek*, and local patterns of gendered consumer power; between the commodification of the body and the muddying of gender boundaries; between the unregulated consumption of pornographic imagery now possible through technologies like the internet and attempts by ordinary men and women to use both narrative and technology to gain greater control over their own lives. At the same time, they perhaps also indicate the vanishing-point of some of our most cherished assumptions: in the K/S world gay and straight, male and female, public and private seem to fold in upon each other and threaten to implode. Neither is quite thinkable without the other, yet as we boldly go into the era of electronic reproduction with its associated struggles around freedom of communication and access, no one can be quite sure precisely where the new frontier of gender truly lies.

CONCLUSION

'Gender ought not to be construed as a stable identity', writes Judith Butler. Instead, it should be seen as an 'effect', the 'mundane' product of regularly repeated 'bodily gestures, movements, and styles of various kinds' that create the impression of 'an abiding gendered self', to cite once more a passage that was quoted earlier (Butler 1990: 140). As we saw in the Introduction, Butler calls this impression an 'illusion' because she wants to underline the tenuous way in which gender is routinely realized through those performances that allow it to be identified or recognized for what it is, performances that are open to disruption, unexpected variation and transformation. Put like this, gender is apt to sound hollow, insubstantial, lacking in psychic depth; but Butler's point is that ultimately gender is only as solid as the social and cultural practices that constitute it over time.

Butler's emphasis upon the performative character of gender echoes a number of contemporary trends: the deliberate theatricality of issue-based political movements like Queer Nation, fashionable and typically gender-ambiguous forms of body-art such as tattooing and piercing, the increasing public visibility of erotic minorities including transsexuals and transvestites. Her formulations seem to capture the fluidity and expressiveness currently displayed by gendered bodies, our belief in their plasticity and adaptability, the difficulties we face in 'reading' identity from appearances. Under such a regime of difference the putative distinction between sex and gender is frequently haphazard or obscured, just as the new signification of 'queer' discussed in Chapter 4 points to a blurring of the lines between heterosexual, gay, lesbian and bisexual practices.

Throughout this book gender has figured as a chameleon-like category, a name for a constantly changing phenomenon that can sometimes be more and also sometimes rather less than an identity: a system of hierarchical relationships, for example, or at the other extreme, the glimpse or trace of a style on a busy urban street. This is not to say that gender has not historically been a major component of people's sense of who they are or what they would like to be. But it has not always been understood as the naturally occurring foundation of an identity. For, as Judith Halberstam has recently argued, gender has varied according to a number of different principles in both modern and pre-modern societies. In some circumstances what Halberstam calls 'gender variance' may be determined primarily by a woman's marital status or its absence (the nineteenth-century 'spinster'); in other instances, like transsexualism or hermaphroditism, it may be directly 'measured on the body' (Halberstam 1998: 59).

Halberstam's challenging study *Female Masculinity* is exemplary for its insistence upon the multiplicity of forms that gender can take, refusing to lump them all carelessly together. But her arguments take us to the limits of present-day gender theory. Halberstam's book is based upon the premise that women themselves have helped to create modern masculinity, not just via the contrast with femininity, but by developing their own unique kinds of masculine personae. Female masculinities have proliferated over the ages and include such different modes as the tomboy, the female husband, the stone butch and the drag king, to cite just a few. As their names suggest, these types are linked to particular roles or performances and are not necessarily defined by their sexual preferences. Halberstam notes that 'some rural women may be considered masculine by urban standards', yet 'their masculinity may simply have to do with the fact that they engage in more manual labour than other women' (58). Similarly, her brief discussion of American cowgirls makes the obvious point that their tough self-presentation is partly a product of an intensely physical outdoor lifestyle herding cattle and competing in rodeos. These manifestations of masculinity are not merely imitative, as George Mosse's all-encompassing account of the Western manly ideal discussed in Chapter 2 would lead us to believe; instead, they represent an independent or alternative line of development: 'masculinity without men' (13).

Although, as this last phrase (and indeed the title of her book) indicate, Halberstam sometimes seems to want to unify these disparate identities, claiming at one point that 'female masculinity is a specific gender with its own cultural history', her main concern is to complicate and unravel our existing preconceptions (77). So, from her perspective, lesbianism is too loose a catch-all to do justice to the variety of positions that historically have been available and consequently it is a descriptor that is often blind to certain key differences in self-understanding. In her discussion of Radclyffe Hall, for example, Halberstam argues that what the author accomplishes in both her writing and her life is the articulation of 'a complex female masculinity, one that neither copies male homosexuality nor male heterosexuality but that carves out its own gender expression' (90). Against Terry Castle who in her book *Kindred Spirits: Noël Coward and Radclyffe Hall* (1996) has attempted to chart the mutual influences, the hidden commonalities between lesbian and gay male styles in the 1920s, Halberstam contends that Hall embraced the medical definition of the 'masculine invert', a person who experienced herself as, and who looked like a man, but whose body was, according to strict anatomical criteria, female. Like her character Stephen Gordon in *The Well of Loneliness*,

Hall sought to find a mode of dress that would enable her to feel comfortable with herself, yet which stopped short of masquerading as a man, thereby distinguishing herself from the figure of the transvestite or 'the passing woman'. On this reading, both Stephen and Hall (the boundary between character and author tends to be elided here) are portrayed as quintessentially modern gendered selves who see their identity not as 'organically emanating from the flesh but as a complex act of self-creation in which the dressed body' rather than the naked or undressed body, 'represents one's desire' (Halberstam 1998: 106).

There is a discernible tension in the argument at this stage, for as Halberstam clearly recognizes (and as Hall's recently published letters show) she believed that to be an 'invert' was an entirely 'natural' phenomenon, despite the fact that it condemned one to a constant struggle against a blatantly discriminatory world. Indeed, in the 1920s the category of the invert was predicated precisely on its apparent fixity; and, of course, we will never know how many women would have chosen 'gender reassignment' by surgical means if such an option had then been available. Yet elsewhere in her discussion, Halberstam notes that Stephen Gordon's 'feelings about her body' are 'essentially contradictory' and it is as if her choice of clothing (her 'sartorial aesthetic') functions as a cultural solvent of these corporeal anxieties (90, 101). We return therefore not only to the vexed question of the relationship between nature and culture, or to the lived significance of discursive constructs and systems of classification, but to the problem of how far change is possible, and the extent to which gender can be imagined otherwise. For gender is never wholly protean nor totally fluid; at any given time and place it is configured within a range of technological, socio-economic and cultural constraints. And though these constraints may mark the discursive limits of our world, they are also the starting point from which our imaginations may defiantly begin again.

BIBLIOGRAPHY

PRIMARY TEXTS

Atwood, Margaret (1986), *The Handmaid's Tale* (Boston: Houghton Mifflin).

Baldwin, James (1985), *The Price of the Ticket: Collected Nonfiction 1948–1985* (New York: St Martin's Press/Marek).

—— (1990), *Giovanni's Room* (Harmondsworth: Penguin).

Barnes, Djuna (1961), *Nightwood* (New York: New Directions).

Barrett Browning, Elizabeth (1996), *Aurora Leigh*, ed. Margaret Reynolds (New York: W.W. Norton).

Beyle, Henri (1955), *The Private Diaries of Stendhal*, ed. and trans. Robert Sage (London: Gollancz).

Boswell, James (1950), *Boswell's London Journal 1762–1763*, ed. and intro. Frederick A. Pottle (London: Heinemann).

—— (1953), *Life of Johnson* (Oxford: Oxford University Press).

Bowen, Elizabeth (1998), *The Last September* intro. Victoria Glendinning (London: Vintage).

Brontë, Charlotte (1987), *Jane Eyre*, 2nd edn, ed. Richard J. Dunn (New York: W.W. Norton).

Burroughs, William S. (1966), *Junkie* (London: New English Library).

—— (1994), *The Letters of William S. Burroughs 1945–1959*, ed. Oliver Harris (New York: Penguin).

Carlyle, Thomas (1881), *Reminiscences*, Vol.1 (London: Longmans, Green).

—— (1966), *On Heroes, Hero-Worship and the Heroic in History* (Lincoln NE: University of Nebraska Press).

—— (1971), *Selected Writings*, ed. Alan Shelston (Harmondsworth: Penguin).

Craik, Dinah Mulock (2000), *Olive*, ed. and intro. Cora Kaplan (Oxford: Oxford University Press).

Dickens, Charles (1982), *Dombey and Son* (Oxford: Oxford University Press).

Du Maurier, Daphne (1992), *Rebecca* (London: Arrow).

Firestone, Shulamith (1979), *The Dialectic of Sex: the Case for Feminist Revolution* (London: Women's Press).

Forster, E.M. (1989), *The Life to Come and Other Stories*, ed. and intro. Oliver Stallybrass (Harmondsworth: Penguin).

Freud, Sigmund (1973–86), *The Penguin Freud Library*, 15 vols. ed. Angela Richards (1973–82) and Albert Dickson (1982–86), (Harmondsworth: Penguin).

Gaskell, Peter (1972), *The Manufacturing Population of England, Its Moral, Social and Political Conditions, and the Changes Which Have Arisen from the Use of Steam Machinery; with an Examination of Infant Labour* (New York: Arno Press).

Gide, André (1960), *The Immoralist*, trans. Dorothy Bussy (Harmondsworth: Penguin).

Gissing, George (1994), *The Collected Letters of George Gissing, Volume Five: 1892–1895* ed. Paul F. Mattheisen *et al.* (Athens OH: Ohio University Press).

Hall, Radclyffe (1990), *The Well of Loneliness* (New York: Anchor).

Harper, Frances Ellen Watkins (1987), *Iola Leroy* (Boston: Beacon Press).

Hornby, Nick (1992), *Fever Pitch* (London: Gollancz).

Hurston, Zora Neale (1937) *Their Eyes Were Watching God* (Philadelphia PA: J.B. Lippincott).

Joyce, James (1964), *Ulysses* (London: Bodley Head).

Jünger, Ernst (1929), *The Storm of Steel: From the Diary of a German Storm-Troop Officer on the Western Front*, trans. Basil Creighton (London: Chatto & Windus).

—— (1993), 'On Danger' [1931], trans. Donald Reneau, *New German Critique* 59: 27–32.

Kafka, Franz (1992), *The Transformation ('Metamorphosis') and Other Stories*, trans. Malcolm Pasley (Harmondsworth: Penguin).

Kinsey, Alfred C., Wardell B. Pomeroy and Clyde E. Morton (1948), *Sexual Behavior in the Human Male* (Philadelphia PA: W.B.Saunders).

Krafft-Ebing, Richard von (1904), *Textbook of Insanity Based on Clinical Observations* (Philadelphia PA: F.A.Davis).

Larsen, Nella (1986), *Quicksand* and *Passing*, ed. Deborah E. McDowell (New Brunswick: Rutgers University Press).

LeGuin, Ursula K.(1977), *The Left Hand of Darkness* (St Albans: Panther).

Nashe, Thomas (1972), *The Unfortunate Traveller and Other Works*, ed. J.B.Steane (Harmondsworth: Penguin).

Paré, Ambroise (1634), *The Workes of that famous Chirurgion Ambrose Parey*, trans. Thomas Johnson (London: Th.Cotes and R.Young).

Piercy, Marge (1976), *Woman on the Edge of Time* (New York: Alfred A. Knopf).

Remarque, Erich Maria (1993), *All Quiet on the Western Front*, trans. A.W.Wheen (London: Picador).

Steele, Richard and Joseph Addison (1982), *Selections from The Tatler and The Spectator* ed. Angus Ross (Harmondsworth: Penguin).

Ward, Edward (1756), *A Compleat and Humorous Account Of All the Remarkable Clubs and Societies in the Cities of London and Westminster* 7th edn (London: J.Wren).

Warhol, Andy (1977), *The Philosophy of Andy Warhol (From A to B and Back Again)* (New York: Harcourt Brace).

—— (1989), *The Andy Warhol Diaries*, ed. Pat Hackett (New York: Warner Books).

Wilmot, John Earl of Rochester (1994), *The Complete Works*, ed. Frank H. Ellis (Harmondsworth: Penguin).

Winterson, Jeanette (1996), *Art Objects: Essays on Ecstasy and Effrontery* (London: Vintage).

Wittig, Monique (1964), *L'Opoponax* (Paris: Editions de Minuit).

—— (1969), *Les Guérillères* (Paris: Editions de Minuit).

—— (1979), *The Opoponax*, trans. Helen Weaver (London: Women's Press).

—— (1992), *The Straight Mind and Other Essays* (Hemel Hempstead: Harvester Wheatsheaf).

Wollstonecraft, Mary (1976), *The Wrongs of Woman, or Maria* (London: Oxford University Press).

—— (1988), *A Vindication of the Rights of Woman*, 2nd edn, ed. Carol H. Poston (New York: W.W. Norton).

Woolf, Virginia (1973), *A Room of One's Own* (Harmondsworth: Penguin).

—— (1979), 'Women and Fiction' in Michèle Barrett, ed., *Virginia Woolf: Women and Writing* (London: Women's Press).

—— (1992), *A Woman's Essays: Selected Essays*, Vol. 1, ed. Rachel Bowlby (Harmondsworth: Penguin).

—— (1992), *Orlando*, ed. Rachel Bowlby (Oxford: Oxford University Press).

SECONDARY TEXTS

Allen, Carolyn (1993), 'The Erotics of Nora's Narrative in Djuna Barnes's *Nightwood*', *Signs: Journal of Women in Culture and Society* 19: 176–200.

American Psychiatric Association (1994), *Diagnostic and Statistical Manual of Mental Disorders* (DSM-IV), 4th edn (Washington DC: American Psychiatric Association).

Anderson, Mark M. (1992), *Kafka's Clothes: Ornament and Aestheticism in the Habsburg Fin de Siècle* (Oxford: Oxford University Press).

Armstrong, Nancy (1987), *Desire and Domestic Fiction: A Political History of the Novel* (New York: Oxford University Press).

Armstrong, Tim (1998), *Modernism, Technology and the Body: A Cultural Study* (Cambridge: Cambridge University Press).

Bakhtin, Mikhail (1968), *Rabelais and his World*, trans. Helen Iswolsky (Cambridge MA: MIT Press).

—— (1981), *The Dialogic Imagination*, trans. Caryl Emerson and Michael Holquist (Austin: University of Texas Press).

Beauman, Nicola (1995), *A Very Great Profession: The Women's Novel 1914–39* (London: Virago).

Bersani, Leo (1995), *Homos* (Cambridge MA: Harvard University Press).

Boone, Joseph A. (1998), *Libidinal Currents: Sexuality and the Shaping of Modernism* (Chicago: University of Chicago Press).

Bray, Alan (1995), *Homosexuality in Renaissance England* (New York: Columbia University Press).

Butler, Judith (1990), *Gender Trouble: Feminism and the Subversion of Identity* (London: Routledge).

—— (1991), 'Imitation and Gender Insubordination' in Diana Fuss, ed., *Inside/Out: Lesbian Theories, Gay Theories* (New York: Routledge).

—— (1993), *Bodies that Matter: On the Discursive Limits of 'Sex'* (New York: Routledge).

—— (1997), *The Psychic Life of Power: Theories in Subjection* (Stanford CA: Stanford University Press).

Carby, Hazel V. (1987), *Reconstructing Womanhood: The Emergence of the Afro-American Woman Novelist* (New York: Oxford University Press).

Castle, Terry (1996), *Kindred Spirits: Noël Coward and Radclyffe Hall* (New York: Columbia University Press).

Chapman, Guy (1937), *Beckford* (London: Jonathan Cape).

Chauncey, George (1994), *Gay New York: Gender, Urban Culture, and the Making of the Gay Male World 1890–1940* (New York: Basic Books).

Clarke, Norma (1991), 'Strenuous idleness: Thomas Carlyle and the man of letters as hero', in Michael Roper and John Tosh, eds, *Manful Assertions: Masculinities in Britain since 1800* (London: Routledge).

Cohen, Ed (1993), *Talk on the Wilde Side: Toward a Genealogy of a Discourse on Male Sexualities* (New York: Routledge).

Comfort, Alex (1963), *Sex in Society* (London: Duckworth).

Connell, R.W. (1987), *Gender and Power: Society, the Person and Sexual Politics* (Cambridge: Polity Press).

—— (1995), *Masculinities* (Berkeley: University of California Press).

Connor, Steven (1996), *The English Novel in History 1950–1995* (London: Routledge).

Corber, Robert J. (1993), *In the Name of National Security: Hitchcock, Homophobia, and the Political Construction of Gender in Postwar America* (Durham NC: Duke University Press).

Cressy, David (1990), 'Literacy', in Martin Coyle, Peter Garside, Malcolm Kelsall and John Peck, eds, *Encyclopedia of Literature and Criticism* (London: Routledge).

Davidson, Arnold I. (1987), 'Sex and the Emergence of Sexuality', *Critical Inquiry* 14:1, 16–48.

De Lauretis, Teresa (1987), *Technologies of Gender: Essays on Theory, Film, and Fiction* (Bloomington IN: Indiana University Press).

Eagleton, Terry (1984), *The Function of Criticism: From The Spectator to Post-Structuralism* (London: Verso).

Elias, Norbert (1982), *The Civilizing Process*, Vol. 2: *State Formation and Civilization*, trans. Edmund Jephcott (Oxford: Basil Blackwell).

Feuer, Jane (1995), *Seeing Through the Eighties: Television and Reaganism* (London: British Film Institute).

Fish, Stanley (1980), *Is There a Text in this Class? The Authority of Interpretive Communities* (Cambridge MA: Harvard University Press).

Flint, Kate (1993), *The Woman Reader 1837–1914* (Oxford: Clarendon Press).

Foucault, Michel (1979), *The History of Sexuality*, Vol. 1: *An Introduction*, trans. Robert Hurley (Harmondsworth: Penguin).

—— (1980), *Herculine Barbin, Being the Recently Discovered Memoirs of a Nineteenth-Century French Hermaphrodite*, trans. Richard McDougal (New York: Pantheon).

—— (1987), *The Use of Pleasure: The History of Sexuality Volume 2*, trans. Robert Hurley (Harmondsworth: Penguin).

Fowler, Bridget (1991), *The Alienated Reader: Women and Popular Romantic Literature in the Twentieth Century* (London: Harvester Wheatsheaf).

Fuss, Diana (1989), *Essentially Speaking: Feminism, Nature and Difference* (New York: Routledge).

Gilbert, Sandra M. (1980), 'Costumes of the Mind: Transvestism as Metaphor in Modern Literature', *Critical Inquiry* 7: 391–417.

Gilbert, Sandra M.and Susan Gubar (1979), *The Madwoman in the Attic: The Woman Writer and the Nineteenth-Century Literary Imagination* (New Haven CT: Yale University Press).

Glendinning, Victoria (1993), *Elizabeth Bowen: Portrait of a Writer* (London: Phoenix).

Glover, David (1996), 'A Tale of "Unwashed Joyceans": James Joyce,

Popular Culture and Popular Theory' in R.B. Kershner, ed., *Joyce and Popular Culture* (Gainesville: University Press of Florida).

Gombrich, E.H. (1978), *The Story of Art* (London: Phaidon).

Guest, Harriet (1996), 'Modern Love: Feminism and Sensibility in 1796', *New Formations* 28: 3–20.

Habermas, Jürgen (1989), *The Structural Transformation of the Public Sphere: An Inquiry into a Category of Bourgeois Society*, trans. Thomas Burger (Cambridge MA: MIT Press).

—— (1992), 'Further Reflections on the Public Sphere', in Craig Calhoun, ed., *Habermas and the Public Sphere* (Cambridge MA: MIT Press).

Halberstam, Judith (1998), *Female Masculinity* (Durham NC: Duke University Press).

Hansen, Miriam (1983), 'Early Silent Cinema: Whose Public Sphere?' *New German Critique* 29: 147–84.

—— (1991), *Babel and Babylon: Spectatorship in American Silent Film* (Cambridge MA: Harvard University Press).

—— (1993), 'Early Cinema, Late Cinema: Permutations of the Public Sphere', *Screen* 34:3, 197–210.

Haraway, Donna J. (1991), 'A Cyborg Manifesto: Science, Technology, and Socialist-Feminism in the Late Twentieth Century', in *Simians, Cyborgs, and Women: The Reinvention of Nature* (New York: Routledge), 149–81.

Hartley, Jenny (1999), 'Reading in Groups', *Times Literary Supplement* (18 June), 18.

Hovey, Jaime (1997), '"Kissing a Negress in the Dark": Englishness as Masquerade in Virginia Woolf's *Orlando*', *PMLA* 112:3, 393–404.

Huyssen, Andreas (1986), *After the Great Divide: Modernism, Mass Culture and Postmodernism* (London: Macmillan).

—— (1993), 'Fortifying the Heart – Totally: Ernst Jünger's Armored Texts', *New German Critique* 59: 3–23.

Jenkins, Henry (1990), '"If I Could Speak With Your Sound": Fan Music, Textual Proximity, and Liminal Identification', *Camera Obscura* 23: 149–75.

Kaplan, Cora (1986), '*The Thorn Birds*: Fiction, Fantasy, Femininity', in Victor Burgin, James Donald and Cora Kaplan, eds, *Formations of Fantasy* (London: Methuen).

Keating, Peter (1991), *The Haunted Study: A Social History of the English Novel 1875–1914* (London: Fontana).

Kotz, Liz (1992), 'The Body You Want: An Interview with Judith Butler', *Artforum International* 31:3, 82–9.

Kracauer, Siegfried (1995), *The Mass Ornament: Weimar Essays*, ed. and trans. Thomas Y. Levin (Cambridge MA: Harvard University Press).

Kramnick, Jonathan Brody (1997), 'The Making of the English Canon', *PMLA* 112:5, 1087–101.

Lane, Christopher (1999), *The Burdens of Intimacy: Psychoanalysis and Victorian Masculinity* (Chicago: University of Chicago Press).

Laplanche, Jean (1976), *Life and Death in Psychoanalysis*, trans. Jeffrey Mehlman (Baltimore: The Johns Hopkins University Press).

Laqueur, Thomas (1990), *Making Sex: Body and Gender from the Greeks to Freud* (Cambridge MA: Harvard University Press).

Leavis, Q.D. (1979), *Fiction and the Reading Public* (Harmondsworth: Penguin).

Light, Alison (1991), *Forever England: Femininity, Literature and Conservatism between the Wars* (London: Routledge).

Long, Elizabeth (1986), 'Women, Reading, and Cultural Authority: Some Implications of the Audience Perspective in Cultural Studies', *American Quarterly* 38:4, 591–612.

—— (1987), 'Reading Groups and the Postmodern Crisis of Cultural Authority', *Cultural Studies* 1:3, 306–27.

McAleer, Joseph (1992), *Popular Reading and Publishing in Britain 1914–1950* (Oxford: Clarendon Press).

McDowell, Deborah (1986), 'Introduction', Nella Larsen *Quicksand* and *Passing* (New Brunswick: Rutgers University Press), ix–xxxv.

Macey, David (1993), *The Lives of Michel Foucault* (London: Hutchinson).

McKeon, Michael (1995), 'Historicizing Patriarchy: the Emergence of Gender Difference in England, 1660–1760', *Eighteenth-Century Studies* 28:3, 295–322.

McLuhan, Marshall (1969), *The Gutenberg Galaxy* (New York: Signet).

Mayne, Judith (1988), *Private Novels, Public Films* (Athens GA: University of Georgia Press).

Merck, Mandy (1998), 'Savage Nights' in Mandy Merck, Naomi Segal and Elizabeth Wright, eds, *Coming Out of Feminism?* (Oxford: Basil Blackwell).

Meyer, Susan (1996), '"India Ink": Colonialism and the Figurative Strategy of *Jane Eyre*', in *Imperialism at Home: Race and Victorian Women's Fiction* (Ithaca: Cornell University Press).

Millett, Kate (1977), *Sexual Politics* (London: Virago).

Mitchell, Juliet (1974), *Psychoanalysis and Feminism: Freud, Reich, Laing and Women* (London: Allen Lane).

Mosse, George L. (1996), *The Image of Man: The Creation of Modern Masculinity* (Oxford: Oxford University Press).

Mouffe, Chantal (1983), 'The Sex/Gender System and the Discursive Construction of Women's Subordination', in Sakari Haninen and Leena Paldan, eds, *Rethinking Ideology: A Marxist Debate* (Berlin: Argument-Verlag).

Mulvey, Laura (1989), *Visual and Other Pleasures* (Bloomington IN: Indiana University Press).

Neale, Steve (1983), 'Masculinity as Spectacle', *Screen* 24:6, 2–16.

Negt, Oskar and Alexander Kluge (1993), *The Public Sphere and Experience*, trans. Peter Labanyi, Jamie Daniel and Assenka Oksiloff (Minneapolis: University of Minnesota Press.

Nussbaum, Felicity (1989), *The Autobiographical Subject: Gender and Ideology in Eighteenth-Century England* (Baltimore: The Johns Hopkins University Press).

Pacteau, Franchette (1986), 'The Impossible Referent: representations of the androgyne' in Victor Burgin, James Donald and Cora Kaplan, eds, *Formations of Fantasy* (London: Methuen), 62–84.

Penley, Constance (1989), 'Individual Response: The Spectatrix', *Camera Obscura* 20–1: 256–60.

—— (1992), 'Feminism, Psychoanalysis, and the Study of Popular Culture', in Lawrence Grossberg, Cary Nelson and Paula Treichler, eds, *Cultural Studies* (New York: Routledge).

Petro, Patrice (1989), *Joyless Streets: Women and Melodramatic Representation in Weimar Germany* (Princeton NJ: Princeton University Press).

Poovey, Mary (1988), *Uneven Developments: The Ideological Work of Gender in Mid-Victorian England* (Chicago: University of Chicago Press).

Rabinovitz, Lauren (1990), 'Temptations of Pleasure: Nickelodeons, Amusement Parks, and the Sights of Female Sexuality', *Camera Obscura* 23: 71–89.

Radway, Janice (1983), 'Women Read the Romance: the Interaction of Text and Context', *Feminist Studies* 9:1, 53–78.

—— (1987), *Reading the Romance: Women, Patriarchy, and Popular Literature* (London: Verso).

—— (1988), 'Reception Study: Ethnography and the Problems of Dispersed Audiences and Nomadic Subjects', *Cultural Studies* 2:3, 359–91.

Riley, Denise (1988), *'Am I That Name?': Feminism and the Category of 'Women' in History* (London: Macmillan).

Riviere, Joan (1986), 'Womanliness as a Masquerade', in Victor Burgin,

James Donald and Cora Kaplan, eds, *Formations of Fantasy* (London: Methuen).

Roberts, Michael (1999), 'Stealing Beauty', *New Yorker*, 20 September: cover.

Rose, Jacqueline (1986), 'Femininity and its Discontents', in *Sexuality in the Field of Vision* (London: Verso).

Rubin, Gayle (1975), 'The Traffic in Women: Notes on the "Political Economy" of Sex', in Rayna R. Reiter, ed., *Toward an Anthropology of Women* (New York: Monthly Review Press).

Russo, Mary (1995), *The Female Grotesque: Risk, Excess and Modernity* (London: Routledge).

Santner, Eric (1996), 'Kafka's *Metamorphosis* and the Writing of Abjection' in Stanley Corngold, trans. and ed., *The Metamorphosis* (New York: W.W. Norton).

Scott, Joan Wallach (1988), *Gender and the Politics of History* (New York: Columbia University Press).

—— (1996), *Only Paradoxes to Offer: French Feminists and the Rights of Man* (Cambridge, MA: Harvard University Press).

Sedgwick, Eve Kosofsky (1993), *Tendencies* (Durham NC: Duke University Press).

Segal, Lynne (1987), *Is the Future Female? Troubled Thoughts on Contemporary Feminism* (London: Virago).

Segal, Naomi (1998), *André Gide: Pederasty and Pedagogy* (Oxford: Clarendon Press).

Senelick, Laurence (1990), 'Mollies or Men of Mode? Sodomy and the Eighteenth-Century London Stage', *Journal of the History of Sexuality* 1:1, 33–67.

Shevelow, Kathryn (1989), *Women and Print Culture: The Construction of Femininity in the Early Periodical* (London: Routledge).

Showalter, Elaine (1978), *A Literature of their Own: British Women Novelists from Brontë to Lessing* (London: Virago).

Simpson, Mark (1996), *It's a Queer World* (London: Vintage).

Snitow, Ann (1990), 'A Gender Diary' in Marianne Hirsch and Evelyn Fox Keller, eds, *Conflicts in Feminism* (New York: Routledge).

Sontag, Susan (1966), *Against Interpretation and Other Essays* (New York: Delta).

Spivak, Gayatri Chakravorty (1985), 'Three Women's Texts and a Critique of Imperialism', in Henry Louis Gates, Jr., ed., *"Race," Writing and Difference* (Chicago: Chicago University Press).

Stacey, Jackie (1994), *Star Gazing: Hollywood Cinema and Female Spectatorship* (London: Routledge).

Staiger, Janet (1992), *Interpreting Films: Studies in the Historical Reception of American Cinema* (Princeton NJ: Princeton University Press).

Stallybrass, Peter and Allon White (1986), *The Politics and Poetics of Transgression* (Ithaca NY: Cornell University Press).

Stepan, Nancy (1990), 'Race and Gender: The Role of Analogy in Science' in David Theo Goldberg, ed., *Anatomy of Racism* (Minneapolis: University of Minnesota Press).

Stoller, Robert J. (1968), *Sex and Gender: On the Development of Masculinity and Femininity* (London: Hogarth Press).

—— (1996), 'Notes on Foucault', *Psychoanalytic Review* 18:1, 11–20.

Stutfield, Hugh (1897), 'The Psychology of Feminism', *Blackwood's Edinburgh Magazine* 161: 104–17.

Sussman, Herbert (1995), *Victorian Masculinities: Manhood and Masculine Poetics in Early Victorian Literature and Art* (Cambridge: Cambridge University Press).

Taylor, Barbara (forthcoming), *Mary Wollstonecraft and the Feminist Imagination* (Cambridge: Cambridge University Press).

Theweleit, Klaus (1987), *Male Fantasies*, Vol. 1: *Women, Floods, Bodies, History*, trans. Stephen Conway *et al.* (Cambridge: Polity Press).

—— (1989), *Male Fantasies*, Vol. 2: *Male Bodies: Psychoanalyzing the White Terror*, trans. Stephen Conway *et al.* (Cambridge: Polity Press).

Thomas, Kendall (1996), '"Ain't Nothin' Like the Real Thing": Black Masculinity, Gay Sexuality, and the Jargon of Authenticity' in Marcellus Blount and George P. Cunningham, eds, *Representing Black Men* (New York: Routledge).

Thompson, Nicola Diane (1996), *Reviewing Sex: Gender and the Reception of Victorian Novels* (London: Macmillan).

Torres, Enrique R. (1991), 'A Perversion Named Desire', *International Journal of Psycho-Analysis* 72:1, 73–92.

Trumbach, Randolph (1987), 'Sodomitical subcultures, sodomitical roles, and the gender revolution of the eighteenth century: the recent historiography', in Robert P. Maccubin, ed., *'Tis Nature's Fault* (Cambridge: Cambridge University Press).

Tuchman, Gaye and Nina E. Fortin (1989), *Edging Women Out: Victorian Novelists, Publishers, and Social Change* (New Haven CT: Yale University Press).

Wall, Cheryl A. (1995), *Women of the Harlem Renaissance* (Bloomington: Indiana University Press).

Warner, Michael (1990), *The Letters of the Republic: Publication and the*

Public Sphere in Eighteenth-Century America (Cambridge MA: Harvard University Press).

Weed, David (1997/8), 'Sexual Positions: Men of Pleasure, Economy, and Dignity in Boswell's *London Journal*', *Eighteenth-Century Studies* 31:2, 215–34.

White, Jim (1999), 'Queering the Pitch', *The Guardian* G2 (4 March), 2–3.

Whiting, Cécile (1997), *A Taste for Pop: Pop Art, Gender and Consumer Culture* (Cambridge: Cambridge University Press).

Williams, Patricia J. (1991), *The Alchemy of Race and Rights* (Cambridge MA: Harvard University Press).

Williams, Raymond (1965), 'The Analysis of Culture', in *The Long Revolution* (Harmondsworth: Penguin).

—— (1984), 'Charlotte and Emily Brontë', in *The English Novel from Dickens to Lawrence* (London: Hogarth Press).

Worpole, Ken (1983), *Dockers and Detectives* (London: Verso).

INDEX